i

Is
Islam
Tolerant?

Is
Islam
Tolerant?

Dr. Gene A. Youngblood

Conservative
University
Press
Jacksonville, Florida 32258

Is Islam Tolerant?
By: Dr. Gene A. Youngblood

Published by:
Conservative University Press
12021 Old St. Augustine Rd.
Jacksonville, Florida 32258
1-800-GO-BIBLE
www.conservative.edu

Unless otherwise noted, Scripture quotations are from the King James Version of the Bible.

Quotations from the Koran are taken from The Noble Koran, Published by the King Fahd Complex, Madinah, Kingdom of Saudi Arabia

Cover design: Studio-e

International Standard Book Number 978-0-9832115-1-8

Acknowledgement

This book is in part the culmination of years of study, research, prayers and words of encouragement from my wife of 47 years, Dorothy C. Youngblood, Ph.D. I am so blessed to have such a partner in the ministry of research-writing and preaching whereby people are encouraged, educated and enlightened on Biblical, theological, social and political issues.

Special recognition of Rev. Ahmed Allah Jibo, a former Muslim from Africa, a Christian pastor, friend, and doctoral student in Conservative Theological University, Ahmed assisted with some of the research issues and suggestions.

My thanks also for so many that assisted with the manuscript typing, proofing and layout-design work, and for Trish Truesdale's tireless task of typing the manuscript.

A special thanks and recognition goes to my four sons: Gene Jr., Glenn, Greg and Geoff, who have each encouraged and prayed for me throughout the journey of research and the writing of this book.

Preface

"Is Islam Tolerant...?"

If you are unsure how to answer this question, then by all means, read Dr. Gene A. Youngblood's book.

Once upon a time, I thought I had the answers to some other important questions:

- **Is** there an enemy who seeks the utter destruction of our cherished way of life; not for the spoils of war, but to establish a global religion? Surely not!
- **Is** it possible for Americans to be apathetic to the point of selecting leaders who will be complicit as "useful idiots" to enable the destruction of America's founding principles from within? Surely not!
- **Could** the sponsor of the "coexist" bumper stickers be a part of the Islam mafia using propaganda to confuse sheep to sympathize with their ever-increasing demands for speech and religious rights under Sharia law here in America? Surely not!
- **Does** a true Muslim believer in America have to renounce the Constitution and the Judeo-Christian basis of American rule of law? Surely not!
- **Is** the current call for the destruction of Israel coming out of Iran from a whacko leader; part of a centuries' old quest? Surely not!

- **Could** the weakness of worshipping at the altar of "political correctness" enable an avowed enemy to infiltrate our institutions, schools, judiciary branch, congress, military AND CHURCHES? Surely not!
- **Would** a Commander-in-Chief sympathize with an avowed enemy of the Constitution, which he took an oath to uphold and defend? Surely not!
- **Is** there a religion that disguises itself as peaceful but really preaches death to all others as a guiding principle for global dominance? Surely not!
- **Would** our son, Todd, rise up to fight back against the Islamic enemy and be killed in action as part of a victorious counterattack on September 11, 2001? Surely not!

Now, for me, **all of these questions have been answered**, but not in the way that my prior experience or understanding had suggested. The time for Americans to wake up and learn about an ever-present grievous threat to our United States of America is at hand.

Read this book. It is not fiction. It is not to be ignored. It is not a work that has an ending...happy or sad...it is about what America can continue to be, or what may become an "ending" for the America that we have been blessed to have for life, liberty and the pursuit of happiness.

David L. Beamer
Father of Todd Beamer
9/11/01, Flight 93

Contents

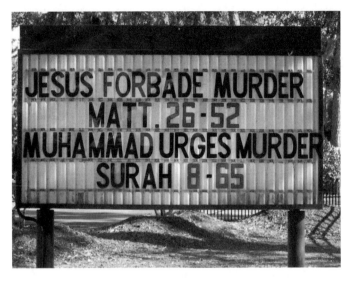

CAMPUS MARQUEE
Located
First Conservative Baptist Church
Conservative Theological University
Jacksonville, FL.

This sign brought confrontation and condemnation by C.A.I.R. and was pictured in newspapers around the world as well as on the internet.

INTRODUCTION

There is a vast amount of confusion, conflict and conversation in society about Islam. Is Islam peaceful? Do the Muslims really want to kill all non-Muslims? Is the Ground Zero Mosque Imam really a peacemaker? Is President Obama and his administration blind, or are they purposefully trying to deceive us? Over 48% of Americans consider Islam to be dangerous to the U.S. I believe God gave America a wake-up call on September 11, 2001, yet we are still hearing different signals. We hear the President and all of the administration making statements like, "Islam is a peaceful religion." This is an orchestrated attempt to make Islam palatable to western ears. The western world and the mind of the average American cannot begin to grasp the big picture of Islam. In his work on Islam, Henry Pike says with simplistic directness, "**Islam is a human time bomb ignited by a hair trigger called hatred**." A Muslim will kill you over his religion and scream "Allah's praise." Islam is poised against all infidels, (i.e.) every non-Muslim. There are multitudes of illustrations and cases where Muslims have killed wives, daughters, and sons for "the glory of Allah." In these killings, they are said to be "honor killings," simply because the wife, daughter or sister was raped, yet she is killed to keep honor in the family. A Muslim TV station owner in New York cut his wife's head off because she displeased him. The Fort Hood jihadist Major Hassan screamed "Allah Akbar," while killing 13 people, and wounding dozens of others. Major Hassan's professional calling card had S.O.A. printed on it, meaning "Soldier of Allah."

Muslims are the most intolerant people on earth. The Koran directs every Muslim to make no friends or alliances with a Christian or Jew, rather they are to slay them; kill them wherever they are found. Muhammad directed that whoever changes his religion, that is leaves Islam, he is to be killed (**Bukhari 9:57**). If a Muslim discontinues his religion, kill him (**Bukhari. 21:260**).

"You can't say that Islam is a religion of peace because Islam does not mean peace. It means submission. So the Muslim is the one who submits. There is a place for violence in Islam. There is a place for Jihad in Islam." **Anjem Choudary, Muslim leader in U.K.**

There is an attempt today to have our society believe that only a small splinter group of radical Muslims are really dangerous. However, when correctly understood, every Muslim that believes the Koran also believes that jihad (murder) is the only valid way for a Muslim to be assured of paradise. **There is a demonic lie that says "true Islam is a peaceful religion,"** everyone is simply getting along with everyone. Our political leadership, including President Obama (of whom I believe to be Muslim), as well as the media, continue with half-truths and misinformation about the dangers of Islam. One only needs to review the true history of Islam to quickly understand that Islam has its roots in hatred and murderous jihad. This has been the history of Islam since Muhammad.

Muhammad was a demon-possessed pedophile, motivated by an evil, wicked rejection of Christians and Jews. He was illiterate (could not read or write). Thus, all of the Koran is simply the result of oral communication between the followers of Muhammad. Muslims around the globe simply hear and heed the words of the Imams as they scream jihad from the mosques around the world. There are dozens of jihadist training camps in America, yet the C.I.A., Homeland Security and the F.B.I. refuse to publically warn the American people. One would only need to ask Geert Wilder (Chairman, Party of Freedom, The Netherlands), about the terrorists in his country.

This book will look at Islam and Allah, as well as Islam and the Koran. There will also be a review of Islam and the right to change or delete Koranic verses, what Islam thinks about the Christian Bible, Islam and deception, as well as Islam and the Jews. Furthermore, we will look at Muhammad as a sinner; there will be a review of Islam and Mary, Salvation, Hell, the Trinity, and what Islam thinks about truth and dialogue. We will see how Islam treats women and their view of polygamy and human rights. We will answer the question; "**Is Islam tolerant**?" Does Islam really teach jihad or killing as a means of being assured a place in paradise?

Islam sees America, the western world, and all Christians and Jews as the enemy that are to be destroyed, thereby pleasing Allah. **Islam is not a peaceful religion**; the Koran is a demonic, dangerous book. In the book, "**Son of Hamas**," the son of the founder of Hamas, Mosab Hassan Yousef; now a Christian, says "**the Koran should be banned in America**." Muhammad was demon-possessed, and Islam has a demonic goal of worldwide domination in the 21st century. Islam now dominates most of Europe and is on the advancing march to control America. **America must wake up before it's too late**.

Every American patriot, preacher, politician and Christian should be aware of the truth of Islam. Believers in Christ should have the knowledge to defend the faith once delivered to the saints. Believers must know the truth of Islam, but most of all, there must be a willingness to study, pray, and be salt and light in a darkened, decaying world as we go out to battle Satan and his demons. Believers must know The Word, and also know the enemy; "Islam," which is Satan's tool in the world today.

Iran's Ayatollah Khomeini said, "**The purest joy of Islam is to kill and be killed for Allah.**" This was made clear on the morning of September 11, 2001, at which event every American, whether they realized it or not, was introduced to the religion or ideology called "Islam." Every Muslim who believes the Koran and earnestly follows the dictates of their religion are without reservation working to bring about world conquest for Islam without regard as to the cost and destruction of all others. **Destruction of America is top priority for Islam, since America is viewed as "the great Satan."** America must awaken before it is too late, Christians must become educated to the truths of Islam and how to respond to its assertions, and claims of tolerance.

There are a few Muslims in America that will not be in agreement with what is written in this book, however, this disagreement is as a result of political correctness. These so-called "moderate" Muslims will not break the commands as set forth in their Koran. **Thus, they are both ideologically and theologically in full agreement with what the Islamic Jihadists are doing**, regardless of what they may assent in an interview or before a T.V. camera on the evening news.

When a Muslim says he wants "peace," you must realize that in Islam, peace only comes when the world is brought into full submission to "Islam." Islam means submission to Allah, not peace as some Muslims try to convince us today, but through global submission to Islam, Muslims believe there will be peace. Imam Faisal Abdul Rauf, the mastermind behind "Cordoba House," the planned ground zero mosque, said on national news, "We want peace." Sure, they want control of America.

Islam and the "ground zero mosque" is a slap in the face of all Americans. 9-11 is the salvo fired across the bow of American freedom and a **full declaration of war**. Multitudes of Americans cannot understand why Islamics have fought so hard to get the political, social and religious approvals to proceed with the mosque. Why ground zero?It is simply because in the 1,400 year history of Islam, the Muslims want a monument, a memorial marker of their success and/or a benchmark as to their failures in Islam. It was September 11, 1689, the day when Islam in their march toward world domination, the day the Muslim jihadists were turned back in their quest for global control met resistance and the Muslims had to retreat because of an alliance of Christian armies. Led by Jan III Sobieski, the King of Poland, they faced Islamic terrorists at the gates of Vienna.

In the minds of the Islamics, this particular September 11th is still frozen in time. It is a day when their vision for world conquest was stopped.Therefore, September 11, 2001 at ground zero, the Pentagon, and a quiet field in Pennsylvania, the Islamic jihad (Holy War) is once again on the march for global conquest and control via Sharia law. Wake up America, before it's too late.

DESTRUCTION OF AMERICA IS TOP PRIORITY FOR ISLAM, SINCE AMERICA IS VIEWED AS "THE GREAT SATAN."

1

Islam and **ALLAH**

Muslims say Allah is merely the Arabic name for God, however, the whole story in pre-Islamic paganism is that there were 360 idols, false gods worshipped in Mecca at the time of Muhammad. Allah is considered the supreme god of the Quraish tribe from which Muhammad came. The father of Muhammad was called Abdu-Allah, which means slave to Allah. This validates the concept that the god, Allah, has its roots in pagan gods. In other words, Allah in fact is the pagan moon god; a dominant deity in pagan Arabia. The crescent moon is a symbol of Islam, and Muslims use the lunar calendar. Muhammad selected the "false" god, "Allah" and rejected all the other false gods.

The Quraish tribe had a custom of praying five times a day in the direction of Mecca, and made pilgrimages to Mecca. They also had a sacred month known as Ramadan dedicated to Mecca. These things are an integral part of the Islamic faith and such practices also tie Islam to pre-Islamic paganism in the modern world. Most Muslims recognize that Allah is not the God of the Bible, however, many immature, unlearned Christians and some evangelicals are attempting to make the claim for the purpose of appeasement and political correctness. They simply are afraid of offending anyone, thus avoiding the doctrinal truth and absolutes of the Bible. Furthermore, it is grievous to find Biblical authors and so-called Christian scholars that are saying that the God of the Bible and Allah are the same.

Names of Allah

What concept do Muslims have of Allah? Who is he whom they worship and call god? What do Muslims claim?

In his struggle against what he viewed as heathen polytheism in Mecca and its surroundings, Muhammad waged a merciless campaign against all gods, idols and images. He stood firm in his teaching: "**Allah is one! All other gods are nothing!**" He had accepted this basic monotheistic faith of the Jews, who having been exiled from their land by the Romans, were living in the Arabian Peninsula. In fact, Muhammad knew much about the Jewish and Christian faiths as is indicated in the perversions and hatred of such faiths found in the Koran. The Koran is replete with Biblical sounding statements, with names and events appearing to be the same as found in the Bible.

The first half of the Islamic creed makes a sharp distinction between the oneness of God and the claims of religions and magical cults which teach that other gods exist besides Allah. Millions of Muslims daily confess, **"There is no god but Allah!"** This testimony is the very core of the Islamic faith. **Whoever does not submit unconditionally** to this dogma is considered by Muslims as a **godless idolater**. Every **theological belief** or **teaching** that does not **submit** to this principal is **rejected without question**, according to the beliefs of Islam. This is why a Muslim will tell a Christian that **Allah will send them to Hell**.

Muhammad described Allah, with a variety of names. The so-called Islamic scholars have systematized all statements of the Koran about Allah, including his attributes and acts into what they call the **"99 beautiful names of Allah."** The names do not occur with the same frequency in the Koran. Several are mentioned a hundred times, others only once or twice, while some are only implied as you read the words of the Koran. Some of the terms, names or descriptions found in the Koran are as follows:

Allah is the Omniscient One

He hears and sees all. He understands all and encompasses everything. He is omnipotent and his strength is unlimited, with power to both build up and destroy. Sounds like the God of the Bible, doesn't it?

Allah is the Exalted One

Great and immeasurable, magnificent and almighty. No one is equal to him. This could also be said of the true God, but the creator-God of the Bible and Allah-the cult god are not the same.

Allah is the Living One

Ever existing, unending, everlasting, eternal, the first and the last, the one and only one, the incomparably beautiful one. Notice the Biblical tone and sound. It is obvious that Muhammad had knowledge of the Bible.

Allah is the Holy One

He is the true reality and the foundation of everything. Allah is the one who created everything out of nothing by the strength of his word. He brought everything into being, and to him we shall all return. He creates life and causes death. He will raise the dead and unite the universe (all into Islam). You can quickly realize the attempt to paraphrase the Biblical truth about God.

Allah is the Sovereign One

He exalts and he abases. He is the defender and the destroyer. Again, one must realize that perhaps multitudes had presented the truth of the true God to Muhammad.

Allah is the Guide and Tempter

He saves whom he wills and condemns whom he wishes. This, however is contrary to the God of the Bible.

Surah 7:44 "And the dwellers of paradise will call out the dwellers of the fire, (saying): "We have indeed found true what our lord had promised us, have you also found true what your lord promised (warnings)? They shall say: "yes." Then, a crier will proclaim between them, **"the curse of Allah is on the (Zalimun) polytheists (all those who believe in the trinity) and wrongdoers," (all non-Muslims).**

Surah 8:27 "O you who believe (Muslims)! Betray not Allah and his messenger, nor betray knowingly your Amanat (things entrusted to you and duties which Allah has ordained for you).

Allah does not forgive everyone who repents.

Surah 16:35 "And those who joined others in worship with Allah said, " If Allah had so willed, neither we nor our fathers would have worshipped aught but him, without (command from) him." So did those before them. Then are the messengers charged with anything but to convey clearly the message?"

Allah is the Compassionate One

But yet he is also the avenger. He has recorded everything precisely and will be the incorruptible and indisputable witness on the Day of Judgment. He is the best of all judges and will present each man with an exact record of his deeds.

Allah is the All Powerful One

His overwhelming authority could open the door to success or hinder an event. He has everything and everyone under his control. He opens and closes the doors. Nothing takes place without his will. Everything depends directly on him. **This is a sure attempt to paraphrase Christian scripture.**

Allah is the Benevolent One

Faithful and kind to Muslims (Not to non-Muslims). He is a generous giver of all gifts and abilities to Muslims. From him alone comes the provision of all mankind. He who possesses everything makes people wealthy and **protects Muslims who glorify him**. He is favorable to them and will be a guardian over all Muslims who worship, believe and obey the Koran.

Allah is the Forgiving One

He acknowledges those who repent and forgives. He is gracious towards the Muslims and establishes a good relationship with them. But **no Muslim can be certain whether the good attributes** of Allah are directed toward him personally, or whether Allah's harsh and devastating side will eventually strike him. Muhammad himself did not know if he was approved of Allah. Regardless of good works, praying five times a day, or giving to the poor, the Muslim has no assurance of paradise, **with the exception of carrying out Islamic jihad.** The Muslim martyr (one who dies in jihad) is assured that he will go to paradise and will be given 72 black-eyed virgins for eternity.

The names of Allah are generously ascribed to him by Islamicsts in wishful thinking, rather than certainty. His **more oppressive** and **frightening attributes** create *fear* in people and drive them to do everything possible to obey the Koran. Poverty and illness are regarded as signs of Allah's wrath for their hidden sins. By the same token, wealth, success and the **esteem of the community in Muslim society** are taken as indications of favor from the "one alone who makes one rich and honors his worshippers with blessings." There are Muslims who say that "**because we have remained faithful to Allah for 1,400 years, he has rewarded us (Muslims) with the oil.**" Islamists continue to seek political appointments, seats of authority and power to illustrate to the Muslim world Allah's approval on Islam. **Muslims in America are encouraged to run for political office, seek political appointments; get involved in the government for control of our political system**.

Let's just leave all such confusing and frustrating names of Allah and simply ask an ordinary Muslim, "**Tell me, who is your god?** What do you think and feel when you hear the name Allah?" He may possibly smile, spread out his arms and say only, "ALLAH!" The average Muslim will admit that Allah cannot be proven or described. One can only sense him and know about his existence. Then perhaps he may admit this intuitive understanding with the phrase, "ALLAH AKBAR!" **Even when murdering innocent human beings, the Muslim will scream "Allah Akbar;"** Allah is great or praise be to Allah.

Major Nidal M. Hasan, stationed at Fort Hood, Texas murdered thirteen people and in the midst of his act of jihad screamed "**Allah Akbar**." Major Hasan is a U.S. Army physician, yet on his calling card he had (S.O.A.) Servant of Allah. His allegiance to Allah is more powerful than his allegiance to the U.S. Military or America. Why is there only silence regarding this Islamic jihadist? **A Muslim cannot have the allegiance to America or our Constitution; his allegiance is to the Koran and Allah**.

"Allah is greater!" In this statement we find the abridged form of the Islamic creed, which is on the lips of billions of Muslims many times per day. It is broadcast from the Muslim prayer towers forty times per day over shops, schools, homes, factories and government buildings. With this testimony, Khomeini's revolutionary guards ran blindly into the mine fields, knowing they were about to be blown to shreds, in the attempt to protect their leader. The 9/11 Islamic terrorist and other jihadists screamed it also. Yet, this phrase is not a complete sentence. **It does not mean** "Allah is great," or "Allah is the greatest." **It literally means**, "**Allah is greater..**"greater than all other gods or the Christian God. Every reader should then, albeit unconsciously, complete the thought: Allah is...wiser than all philosophers, more powerful than the God of the Bible, stronger than all the atomic and hydrogen bombs in the world and greater than everything known. **Allah is the unique and inexplicable one**—the remote, **vast and unknown god**. This is then to say everything we think about Allah is incomplete; if not wrong altogether. Allah cannot be comprehended. He comprehends us. All of humanity are simply slaves who have only the **directive to worship him in abject fear**. This view is opposite of all we know of the God of the Bible. The Christian God is love, mercy, truth and justice. Believers are admonished to come before His Throne boldly with our petitions.

Islam stands for a renunciation of all religions that prevail in the world, especially Christianity and Judaism. One of the characteristics of Islamic ideology is that for centuries, Allah could not be philosophically described. There was not even a desire to comprehend him and to fathom his being. The recognition and understanding of this brings us to a crucial statement expressed by the Islamic theologian al-Ghazali. He had meditated a great deal on the "99 excellent names of god," and wrote that **these names can mean everything and yet nothing**. One name of Allah can negate another, and the content of one may be included in the next. No one can understand Allah. Devout Muslims therefore can **only worship this unknown, super-dimensional demonic deity and live before him in fear and reverence**, while making certain they observe all the Koran in strict obedience, including

Jihad for the assurance of paradise. Americans and the entire western world simply cannot comprehend the thought process or motivations of the Islamic mind. How can we comprehend murder as an "**instruction**" from God?

Allah and Christian Doctrines

Islam has increased greatly and expanded in the last ten years, especially since 9-11, making a substantial thrust into the cultures of Christianity, Hinduism, communism and the African cults. When we, as Christians, meet Muslims and try to understand them, we should not forget that **they are true worshippers who serve Allah, who serve their god with blind dedication within the full scope and teachings of the Koran.** A Christian should not hate them, but should realize that they are blinded by Satan and worship Satan through the false god, Allah, as commanded in the demonic book, the Koran. Christians should attempt to show them Biblically that they are without Christ; thus lost and will go to Hell, unless they reject Islam and receive Jesus Christ as Redeemer, Savior and the only true God. Emery Esse, a former Muslim, now an active Christian said, **"It was the Biblical teaching of Jesus' love that caused me to say yes to Jesus."** However, as Christians, we must seek the truth about Islam, and to present the Biblical truth of Christianity. We need to compare the Koran with the Holy Bible, which is for us, the only standard of truth. When we compare the so-called 99 names of Allah in Islam with the names of God in the

Bible, we must acknowledge that Allah of Islam is not in harmony with our Christian God. Therefore, if a Muslim says, "Your God and our god are the same," either he does not understand who Allah and Christ really are, or he intentionally glosses over the deeply rooted differences. Muslims in America will attempt to deceive the Christian by making such claims; deceit and lies are okay in Islam, if the lie can cause one to believe in Islam, or accept the Muslim position on an issue. The Malaysian government is in an ongoing court case to prove that only Muslims have the constitutional right to use the name "Allah," proving that Muslims believe Allah is a "different" god.

The Trinity Rejected

It is **unthinkable** and impossible for a **Muslim** to **believe in the existence of God as Father**, **Son** and **Holy Spirit** of the New Testament. Islam completely rejects the Holy Trinity, **Surah 5:116; Surah 5:73-75**.

Whoever says that Allah has a partner, companion or an equal God beside him will, from an Islamic point of view, fall into an unforgivable sin *(like the sin against the Holy Spirit in Christianity)*. **Islam firmly rejects the deity of Christ and the deity of the Holy Spirit.** Allah in Islam is always **only one** and **never a unity of three**, even if such a unity was complete in itself. When Christians claim that their Trinity does not mean three different, separated persons, **but a unity in a Trinity** (the Tri-unity of God), **Muslims must repudiate this concept**. For them Allah is never a triune God, but one person alone. For the believers; NO Christ, there is NO Christianity, for Jesus Christ is God come in the flesh, **"the God-man."**

Allah - No Father

As believers, we must remember that in the New Testament, the name "**Father**" is found a minimum of 164 times in the gospels. Jesus Christ is God come in the flesh. He is 100% God and 100% man, yet without sin. It is Jesus that created all things (**Colossians 1:13-18**).

Christ did not preach about a distant, unknown God of whom no one can know or comprehend, nor did he teach us to come in trembling fear before him as the unapproachable holy Judge. As believers we are to come before Him boldly (**Hebrews 4:16**). The veil before God in the Old Testament has been lifted to reveal God as He really is - the Father. He did not teach us to pray to Him in any other name than "Our Father." Christ thus shared his own privilege with us, that through him we have become the children of God, a relationship which Muhammad and all of Islam emphatically rejects. A relationship that no Muslim can have without Jesus as Savior.

Surah 5:18 "And (both) the Jews and the Christians say: 'We are children of Allah and his loved ones.' Say 'why then does he punish you for your sins?' Nay you are but human beings of those he has created, he forgives whom he wills and he punishes whom he wills. And to Allah belongs the dominion of the heavens and the earth and all that is between them and to him is the return (of all)."

Recall that Jesus was challenged by His enemies as relates to God, The Father:

Matthew 26:63 "I adjure you by the living God, that you tell us if you are the Christ, the Son of God."

Caiaphas was unable and unwilling to call God "Father," because to the Jews it would have been slanderous talk. Therefore, he asked Jesus if he considered himself to be the "Son of God", implying the Fatherhood of God. Christ confirmed the validity of his confession. His first words from the cross were, "*Father*, forgive them, for they do not know what they are doing." But as the Father turned His face away in His position as the judge of the sins of the world placed on Jesus the Son, the Son cried out, "My God, my God, why have you forsaken me?" Yet Jesus did not reject the reality of God's Fatherhood in the midst of his suffering and death with the words: "**Father**, into your hands I commit my spirit." The name Father, the revelation of God's true reality, is an inseparable element of the Christian faith. God is related to us in the New Testament as our eternal Father. John stated:

1John 3:1 "Behold what manner of love the Father hath bestowed upon us, that we should be called the sons of God: therefore the world knoweth us not, because they knew Him not."

One of the reasons Islam and the Koran has rejected the Holy Trinity along with the Fatherhood of God is because of a complete rejection of its historical teachings. The Muslims believe that the **Trinity consists of Allah the Father, Jesus and Mary**. Every Christian, will refute this error. It is unfortunate that the birth of Jesus by the power of the Holy Spirit through the womb of the Virgin Mary is understood not spiritually but carnally, in Islam. **For a Muslim, it is blasphemy to think or say that Allah had a son through Mary**. God's spiritual Fatherhood remains incomprehensible to the Muslim minds. For them, Allah is the exalted, distant and mysterious god. They do not know or appreciate the nearness of the God of the Bible, who in his love as our Father revealed himself to us in Jesus Christ as stated in (**John 1:18**).

Allah - No Son!

Jesus Christ as the "Son of God," is another subject that outrages every Muslim. Jesus Christ as God in Christianity is completely rejected by Islam. They cannot contemplate a second divine person existing beside Allah. According to Islam, this would mean the possibility of conflict within the Godhead. In Islamic teaching, the Son could rebel against his Father at any moment. Only Allah is the powerful one. In the Koran, Allah is also called **the arrogant** and the **most crafty** of the cunning.

Surah 59:23 "He is Allah beside whom none has the right to be worshipped but he, the king, the holy, the one free from all defects , the giver of security, the watcher over His creatures, the All-Mighty, the compeller, the supreme. Glory be to Allah! (High is he) above all that they associate as partners with him."

Surah 3:54 "…And Allah is the best of those who plot."

Christ's meekness, humility and gentleness, as well as his self-denial, are regarded as weakness in Islam. It is taken as proof that He is not God when Jesus says, "**I am gentle and humble in heart**," or "**The Son can do nothing of himself**," or "**The Father is greater than I**."

For a Muslim, the mystery of the Holy Trinity remains unknown and completely rejected. The Son continually glorified the Father during His life on earth, just as the Holy Spirit glorifies the Son today. The Father honored the Son and seated him on His right hand, while the Son left to the Holy Spirit, the task of building the Church that he purchased with His own blood (**Acts 20:28**). Christ's statement, "**All authority in heaven and on earth has been given to me**," is blasphemy in the ear of a Muslim. For the Muslim, if this were true, Allah would have no more power in his hands. The spirit of Islam as found in the Koran is full of hatred, anger, pride and a demonic spirit of global control. So a Muslim rejects Christ because of His character and who He is. This is why Islam rejects the thought of praying in the name of Jesus. This is why Islam and the A.C.L.U. are waging war against Christianity in America today in every city and state in an attempt to remove "In Jesus' name," from all prayers.

The existence of a Son of God, according to the Koran, would also mean an encroachment upon Allah's sovereignty. Allah forgives **whom** he wants, **when** he wants and **where** he wants. He does not need a lamb (Jesus), a mediator or a cross. **Islamic reasoning declares the crucified Christ unnecessary because Allah does everything alone.** Muhammad's denial of the son-ship of Christ includes the rejection of the **historical fact of the crucifixion.** Without the crucifixion of Jesus, we have no way of redemption, thus no Christianity. Islam simply says without hesitation:

Surah 4:157 "...they killed him not, nor crucified him..."

Therefore, the Jesus of the Koran is not the Jesus of the Bible. If Allah would have allowed the crucifixion of Christ, then Muhammad could also have expected a shameful death during the time of his persecution in Mecca. Instead, he clung to a perceived powerful Allah, who in sovereign majesty, according to the Koran, protects his prophets. In Islam, the cross of Christ would signify a denial of the omnipotence of Allah, **therefore the Cross and The Crucifixion of Christ are all rejected in Islam.** No cross, no crucifixion, no Christ of Christianity in Islam. Contrary to some denominational teachings today, Islam is **not** a "<u>sister religion</u>" to Christianity.

The contrast between the holiness of God that demands the death of all who are guilty, and **his love that longs to save all sinners, is not found in Islam. Allah**

does not love sinners *(a principle that is recorded 24 times in the Koran),*

Surah 2:190 "And fight in the way of Allah those who fight you, but transgress not the limits. Truly, Allah likes not transgressors" (i.e. all non-Muslims).

This Surah is the first one that was revealed in this connection but it was supplemented by another:

Surah 9:36 "...That is the right religion, so wrong not yourselves therein, and fight against the (polytheists, pagans and idolators, disbelievers in the oneness of Allah) collectively as they fight against you collectively. But know that Allah is with those who are the pious."

For this reason, **no Muslim can ever be certain whether Allah has prepared a place for him in paradise or if the gates of hell will stand wide open to receive him.** What a miserable life to live without the assurance of Heaven! In Islam there is no assurance of salvation or eternal life.

Islam does **not recognize a crucified Son of God**. Without a crucified Christ for all sins and the belief by faith, Muslims will die and go to a devil's Hell. They have no concept of Jesus Christ as the Lamb of God, who became the vicarious sacrifice for mankind, and gave Himself so we can live. Therefore, no Muslim can perceive or receive redemption; they remain without grace, without hope and abide in their sins. The concept and fact of "being saved through Christ" is non-existent in Islam. **The**

true Savior is rejected in the Koran, thus hidden from the eyes and hearts of Muslims.

Allah - No Holy Spirit

Islam rejects not only the Father and the Son, but also denies the Holy Spirit is God but is simply a created spirit; like angels and demons. **The Holy Spirit is said to be the angel Gabriel, who delivered messages from Allah to Mary and Muhammad.** Yet, Muhammad admitted to his wife that he believed demons spoke to him in his initial encounters in a cave. The fact that God is spirit and became flesh in Christ and now lives within the believers is a rejected truth to all of Islam. Without faith and trust in the finished work of Christ on the cross, no person can be saved.

Muslims do not recognize the Holy Spirit and reject the Biblical truth of the indwelling of the Holy Spirit. Therefore, **they cannot call Christ, Lord, and are not saved through Him (1 Corinthians 12:3; Romans 8:9).** A person in whom the Holy Spirit does not dwell has no assurance of answered prayer, no assurance of salvation, or eternal life. **The actual assurance of salvation, is absent in Islam.**

Ask a Muslim if his sins are forgiven, at best you may receive the answer, "If Allah wishes!" **No Muslim knows for sure if this is the will of Allah.** On the other hand, we as Christians can testify, "Yes, God has forgiven all our sins, because his Son bore our guilt and became the payment for all our sins on the cross." The Comforter, the Holy Spirit, testifies with our spirits and hearts that we are justified and have been received into the family of God (**Romans 8:16; Ephesians 2:18-22**).

How then can some Christian theologians claim or declare, "Allah in Islam is identical to God in Judaism and Christianity?" Have they not read the New Testament that says, "He who has the Son has life, he who does not have the Son of God does not have life" (**1 John 5:12**)? Whoever does not identify himself with the cross of Christ does not have eternal life. "For God so loved the world that he gave his only Son, that whosoever believes in him shall not perish, but have eternal life" (**John 3:16**). When the Holy Spirit does not dwell in a person he cannot have eternal life. **No Muslim can be sure that he has eternal life, because he does not accept Christ who is "the life". All that remains for him is judgment and condemnation, while the followers of Christ are delivered from judgment because of His death (John 3:18), and acceptance of His shed blood as full payment.**

Allah - No Love

Our search into the Person of God in both Islam and Christianity boils down to a comparison. We know that God of the Bible is love. Islam acknowledges Allah to be the Merciful One. Perhaps you may ask, "Isn't this name, which occurs in the Koran more than any other name, equivalent to love?" No, not at all.

Aren't mercy and love the same?" Perhaps an illustration can help to clarify the comparison between these two words. Someone used the illustration; if a groom would say to his bride, "**I have mercy on you** and will marry you," what would her reaction be? She would run away from him! But if he says, **"I love you,"** then the relationship will be as it should be. Even in his mercy, which is Islam's favorite name for Allah, he remains the Great and Exalted One who at best will **condescend a little to help his needy creatures**. Even in exercising his mercy he remains **distant** and **impersonal**; no Muslim can truly know him or have the assurance of salvation.

Our God, the Christian God, the God of the Bible, on the other hand, in his love came down to man in the person of Jesus Christ. He took on the form of a man and abased himself to the lowest level, bearing our guilt and taking our place in judgment, (**Philippians 2:5-11**). His self-sacrifice for every sinner is evidence of eternal Holy Love. We do not have a distant impersonal God, but the Father, the Son and the Holy Spirit, who does not hesitate to save us and dwells in us, (**Hebrews 4:13**). Everyone does not recognize or accept the Triune God-Head shows that the true God unknown to him. Belief in the tri-unity of the God-Head is a cardinal doctrine in Christianity. **Thus,**

Muslims are without hope of salvation or heaven, without Jesus Christ!!

The Real Allah

Muslims claim that **Allah** inspired Muhammad and revealed his words and commands to him. Every sentence in the Koran is supposedly the pure word of Allah, infallibly by the almighty. In fact, most if not all of the Koran, is simply distortions and paraphrases or perversions of the Old and New Testaments. The Muslims accept the Old and New Testaments as being inspired by Allah as long as there is **not any conflict in them with the Koran**. All statements in the Bible that are not in agreement with the Koran are considered false, invalid and corrupt, therefore rejected completely by all Muslims. Islam says the Christian's Bible is corrupt and without authority.

An Unbiblical Spirit

We should bear in mind that Islam is a post-Christian religion, over 600 years after the birth of the church. Out of necessity, Muhammad had to come to terms with the Christ of the New Testament. He accepted Christ partially, yet denied that He is God come in the flesh and died on the cross for our sins. This is acceptance only philosophically. We find that the Koran bears clear witness to the virgin birth of Christ, but denies that He was **conceived** of the Holy Spirit. It is evident in the Koran that Islam has no real concept of the virgin birth. Muhammad claims that the Son of Mary was **created** through God's word out of nothing. Jesus' validity in Islam according to the Koran is simply as a great prophet who did mighty wonders. He made the blind to see, healed the lepers and raised the dead. **Without dying, Christ was supposedly lifted by Allah directly into Heaven where He still lives today, and will one day return to assist the hidden Imam in bringing all the world to Islam**. He will come again to judge all Jews and Christians who have not accepted Islam. **According to the Koran, Jesus was not the Son of God, and His crucifixion never took place.**

The Christology of Islam is a **false standard** that they use to measure the Christian's Savior and His salvation. If Islam claims that Muhammad received real inspiration, **then it was another spirit, a false spirit, a demon spirit** and **not** the **Holy Spirit** who **inspired Muhammad**. God does not lie!! Muhammad himself told his wife that he believed demons were speaking to him. Therefore, based on Muhammad's own words we must conclude that Muhammad was in fact demon possessed and inspired of Satan. **This could only mean that the Koran is to be rejected as having no valid spiritual significance.** In fact, all of Islam as seen in the Koran is in direct conflict and in opposition to all we believe as Christians.

The New Testament and Islam

The apostle John wrote in his first epistle:

28

1 John 4:3 "every spirit that does not confess that Jesus Christ has come in the flesh...is the spirit of the antichrist.."

Therefore, we must confess with all humility, and yet with authority, that the spirit in Islam is **the spirit of the antichrist**. Muhammad had heard much about Jesus, but in spite of all, he rejected the crucified Son of God.

The spirit who calls himself Allah and claims to have inspired Muhammad cannot be the Father, our Lord Jesus Christ. Instead, he is a **lying spirit**. The **Allah of Islam is an unclean spirit of Satan, who rules with great power in a religious disguise to this very day (John 8:30-48).** Islam is wicked, evil, dangerous, and will ultimately doom every soul that adheres to its teachings. Every believer has the mandate of Scripture to warn the world of the evil, wicked nature of Islam and the looming destruction of our nations around the world.

"FIGHT AGAINST THEM (NON-MUSLIMS) SO THAT ALLAH WILL PUNISH THEM BY YOUR HANDS AND DISGRACE THEM AND GIVE YOU VICTORY OVER THEM."
SURAH 9:14

2

Islam and **THE KORAN**

The basis for all of Islamic doctrines, ideology, theology and Muslim's total way of life are found in the Koran. Dr. Kenneth Boa, in his book on cults and world religions, describes the central place of the Koran in the Islamic faith as well as the supplementary works:

> "The Koran is the authoritative scripture of Islam. About four-fifths the length of the New Testament, it is divided into 114 Surahs (chapters). Parts were said to be written by Muhammad, (however Muhammad could not read or write), and the rest, based on oral teachings, was written from memory by his disciples (clan followers) after Muhammad's death."

Every Muslim submits to the directives, commands and teachings of the Koran for every aspect of their total life. The Koran is divided into 114 surahs (chapters), contains about 6,200 verses and 330,000 letters, all arranged without chronological order. All supposedly divine, however, there is no evidence of any divinity, for there are no manuscripts and no parchments by which textual critics may examine the words of Gabriel from which (according to Muhammad) the words were given. Muhammad was convinced that it was in fact demons talking to him as he stayed for long hours, even days in a cave. According to Islam, the Koran's revelations were given to Muhammad from around 610 A.D. until shortly before his death in 632 A.D. These (so-called) revelations lasted about 23 years. Because Muhammad could not read or write, these so-called revelations were passed down to others who wrote them down.

Over the past fourteen hundred years according to Islamic scholars, there have been over three hundred thousand Surahs, most of which were after Muhammad's death. However, different Islamic leaders after Muhammad's death would have their own revelations and thus would update the Koran, omitting some of the Surahs and replacing them with their own revelations.

Oral Transmission

During Muhammad's lifetime, he would tell his followers of his revelations said to be from Gabriel, they would in turn memorize them and tell them to others. As narrated by Uthman bin Affan: the prophet said: "the most superior among you are those who learn the Koran and teach it."

Bukhari 6:106   Narrated Abdullah bin Masud:
     Allah's Apostle said to me: "Recite (of the
     Koran) for me." I said: "Shall I recite it to

you although it had been revealed to you?"
He said: "I like to hear (the Koran) from
others."

Bukhari 6:525 "Narrated Qatada: I asked Anas bin
Malik: "Who collected the Koran at the time
of the prophet?" He replied, "Four, all of
whom were from the Ansar: Ubai bin Ka'b,
Muadh bin Jabal, Zaid bin Thabit and Abu
Zaid."

It is said that after the death of Muhammad, these four
could be consulted and correct each other if there were any
disputes over the words of the Koran as they perceived it to
be.

Written Transmission

The official Koran used by Muslims worldwide appears
to be the product of the third caliph named Uthman. What
most Muslims accept as the "official Koran" was collected
and blessed by Islam about 653 A.D. therefore based on
Muslim opinion. The official Koran date is 653 A.D. as the
date of authorship. The full content of the official Koran are
from the oral traditions as memorized and passed on to each
generation by mouth. **The majority of the oral traditions
were created generations after Muhammad's death. Yet
most Muslims believe it's all from Allah to Muhammad.**

About 200 years after Muhammad's death, the year 840
A.D., Muslim scholars wrote down some of the oral
traditions known as Hadith, (musings and sayings of
Muhammad). The Hadiths recorded by these Muslim

scholars are said to be "accurate" about what Muhammad said and how he lived. Most Muslims accept the Hadith (printed in Arabic-English) in 9 volumes. Muhammad's words in the Hadith could be called his commentary on the Koran, because it affirms the Koranic teachings.

A Few Koranic Teachings

The Koran advocates, or outright teaches terrorism (Jihad), murder, wife-beating, lying, destruction of all non-Muslims, rejection of Christians and Jews, polygamy, and multitudes of other teachings which are contrary to any Christian beliefs or Biblical teachings. Some of these Surahs are as follows:

Surah 3:151 "We shall cast terror into the hearts of those who disbelieve (non-Muslims)..."

Surah 3:157 "If you are killed or die in the way of Allah (Jihad), you have forgiveness and mercy from Allah..."

Surah 2:190 "Fight in the way of Allah those who fight you."

Surah 2:191 "And kill them (non-believers) wherever you find them...kill them. Such is the recompense of the disbelievers (non-Muslims)."

Surah 2:193 "Fight until there is no more disbelief in Allah."

Surah 2:98 "Whoever is an enemy to Allah and his messengers, then verily, Allah is an enemy to the disbelievers (non-Muslims)."

Surah 2:113 "The Jews and Christians follow nothing (i.e. not on the right religion), Allah will judge between them."

Surah 2:216 "Jihad (Holy fighting in Allah's cause) is ordained for you (Muslims)..."

Surah 2:244 "Fight in the way of Allah..."

Surah 3:19 "Truly the religion of Allah is Islam...whoever disbelieves Allah will judge."

Surah 3:85 "Whoever seeks a religion other than Islam, it will never be accepted..."

Surah 4:56 "Those who disbelieve...we shall burn them in Fire..."

Surah 4:89 "...If they turn back from Islam take hold of them and kill them wherever you find them..."

Surah 4:101 "The disbelievers (non-Muslims) are ever unto you open enemies."

Surah 4:102 "...Allah has prepared a humiliating torment for the disbelievers (non-Muslims)."

Surah 5:51 "O you who believe (Islam) take not the Jews and Christians as friends."

Surah 5:73 "...A painful torment will befall on the disbelievers (non-Muslims) among them."

Surah 8:39 "Fight them (the non believer) until there is no more disbelief in Islam."

Surah 8:55 "The worst moving (living) creatures before Allah are those who disbelieve (non-Muslims)."

Surah 9:5 "...then kill the disbelievers (non-Muslims) wherever you find them, capture them and besiege them, and lie in wait for them in each and every ambush..."

Surah 9:14 "Fight against them (non-Muslims) so that Allah will punish them by your hands and disgrace them and give you victory over them..."

Surah 9:29 "Fight against those who believe not in Allah...and those (Jews and Christians) who acknowledge not the religion of truth (Islam)..."

The Koran and The Pentagon

In a news article from World Net Daily dated September 27, 2006, the Pentagon tasked intelligence analysts to pinpoint what's driving Muslim after Muslim to do the unthinkable. Their finding is "**politically explosive**," it's their "**Holy Book**," the Koran. The Pentagon's intelligence analysis reached the conclusion that Muslim suicide bombers are in fact students of the Koran who are motivated to violence by the teachings of the Koran.

In Islam, it is not how one lives one's life that guarantees spiritual salvation, but how one dies according to the Pentagon's intelligence briefings.

The Koran and The Bible

Based on the Surahs in the Koran, Muslims accuse Christians of having a corrupted Bible. Muslims say that Christians have changed or added to the Bible; both Old and

New Testaments have been corrupted over the ages and are therefore no longer reliable. The Muslims claim that the Koran is the only remaining unadulterated trustworthy source of true religious doctrine. However, the Koran verifies the authenticity of the Bible in several places. Moreover, the accusation of Bible corruption actually undermines Muslim theory. The Christian author, Dr. Lactantius, expresses it quite well here:

> "We begin with what the Koran says about the Bible; many verses actually confirm that it is God's Word and has not been changed."

Here are only a few for example:

Surah 5:43 "But how do they come to you for decision while they have the Torah, in which is the (plain) decision of Allah..."

Surah 5:44 "Verily, we did send down the Torah...therein is guidance and light..."

Surah 5:46 "We sent Jesus...confirming the Torah that which had come before him, and we gave him the Gospel in which is guidance and light..."

Surah 5:68 "(Jews and Christians) you have nothing (as regards guidance) til you act according to the Torah and the Injil (Gospel)..."

Surah 4:136 "Believe in Allah and His messenger (Muhammad), and the book which He has sent down to His messenger (the Koran) and

37

the Scripture which he sent down to those before him(the Bible)..."

Surah 10:94 "If you (Muhammad) are in doubt concerning that which we reveal unto you [i.e. that your name is written in the Torah and the Gospel], then ask those who are reading the Book (Torah and Gospel) before you. Verily, the truth has come to you from your lord. So be not one of those who doubt (it)."

Surah 15:9 "Verily, We, it is we who have sent down the Koran and surely we will guard it (from corruption)."

Surah 6:34 "...and none can alter the words (decisions) of Allah..."

Surah 10:64 "...no change can there be in the words of Allah."

If the Bible was corrupted, was this before or after Muhammad? If before, why does Allah tell Muhammad to refer to a corrupted Scripture for guidance, and why does he say of the Torah and Gospel, "wherein is guidance and light," rather than "wherein there used to be before they were corrupted"? If after, why does the Muslim not accept the Bible since current translations are all based upon manuscripts that pre-date Muhammad?

If it was corrupted, was it done by the Jews or by the Christians (since neither were on speaking terms with the other)?

Surah 2:113 "The Jews said that the Christians follow nothing (i.e. are not on the right religion) and the Christians said the Jews follow nothing (i.e. are not on the right religion), though they both recite the Scripture."

Surah 5:82 "Verily you will find the strongest among men in enmity to the believers (Muslims), the Jews and those who are idolators and you will find the nearest in love to the believers (Muslims) who say 'we are Christians.' That is because amongst them are priests and monks, and they are not proud."

How could they agree to change every single Bible identically? Why was there no record of this happening, and why did nobody try to stop it, or hide all authentic Bibles? Significantly, the early Muslim commentators, (e.g. Bukhari, al-Razi) were all in agreement that the Bible could not be changed since it was God's word. Several centuries passed before Muslims claimed that the Bible had been changed, only after they carefully read the stories in the Koran and noted they were different from those in the Bible. **The verses used to support corruption in the Bible have been totally misinterpreted and misused by Muslims**. For example:

Surah 2:42 "And mix not truth with falsehood, nor conceal the truth [i.e. Muhammad is Allah's messenger and his qualities are written in

> your Scriptures, the Torah and the Gospel],
> while you know (the truth)."

"Confound truth with falsehood, nor knowingly conceal the truth." The story is told of Muhammad that after two Jews were brought to him for judgment, having committed adultery. The other Jews wanted to test him to see if he was a prophet of God, or if he knew what was in the Torah. So he asked for a Torah, and got a boy to read the punishments for disobedience. When the boy reached **Leviticus 20:10** ("If a man commits adultery with another man's wife...both must be put to death"), the Jew accused of adultery slammed his hand over the verse so the boy could not read it (according to Abu Dawood). A far cry from corrupting the text of the Bible. Other verses say that a group of Jews used to listen to Scripture, then change it—but it was only a group, not all the Jewish people in the world, let alone Mecca. **Second**, they must have had the original genuine copies in order to have been accused of changing it and **third**, they did not change the written text. They could have simply told Muhammad that the Torah said things which were not there in order to mislead him. **Muslims worldwide simply reject the Christian Bible as being the revealed, inspired word of God without error or mixture**.

As with the straw men discussed earlier, it is helpful to be able to show Muslims clearly that the Bible has not been changed and that it is still the authentic Word of God, without error and authentic in every part, because it is God breathed. **Every Christian is responsible to know The Word of God and defend The Word without apology**.

The Koran should be seen in its true color as a compendium of constant, continual, and total "**war**" against all infidels (non-Muslims) both globally and especially in America. The Jihadists of Islam has always felt self-righteous and believed fervently that they are carrying out the commandments of Allah when they commit Holy War (Jihad) as prescribed by Muhammad.

"IF WE ABROGATE A VERSE OR
CAUSE IT TO BE FORGOTTEN, WE
WILL REPLACE IT BY A BETTER
ONE OR SIMILAR."

SURAH 2:106

"ALLAH BLOTS OUT WHAT HE
WILLS AND CONFIRMS (WHAT HE
WILLS). AND WITH HIM IS THE
MOTHER OF THE BOOK."

SURAH 13:39

3

Islam and **ABROGATION**

The doctrine of abrogation, that is of one Koranic passage canceling another, has always been very real, but controversial. From the time Muhammad introduced it to this day, Muslims have been discussing and arguing its truth, validity, contexts, applications and ramifications and **for the most part denying it completely**. This doctrine is significant because **it affects how violence in Islam is applied.** Thus, this crucial aspect of Islamic teaching **must be understood** in order to understand the reasoning behind violence in Islam. When a Muslim is confronted with a Surah from the Koran that teaches jihad, holy war, killing, he will try to tell you that it applies to some Muslim war, etc. He will tell you that you just don't understand the Koran, and will show you another Surah that supposedly rejects jihad, or other Surahs in question.

According to Muhammad, he claims that he heard from the Angel Gabriel, and what the Angel said by Allah, repeated to him (Muhammad). And in turn, Muhammad repeated it to his friends, thus, ultimately forming the Koran.

During his 23 year role as a prophet-leader of Islam, he forgot part of the Koran, and some Koranic Surahs contradicted others' instructions. Teachings and ideologies or doctrines were occasionally at odds. The lack of consistency, the contradictions, and the capricious light that it cast Allah in were very obvious. Various people in Muhammad's time cursed and rejected him, and to counter these critics, Muhammad said that some Koranic Surahs were replaced by other Surahs such as the following Surah.

Surah 2:106 "Whatever a Verse (revelation) do We abrogate or cause to be forgotten, We bring a better one or similar to it. Know you not that Allah is able to do all things?"

Examples of Abrogation

Koranic directives themselves may be abrogated as has occurred in a several places. An example of this abrogation is **Surah 24:2,** which abrogates the punishment of adultery stated in **Surah 4:15-16.** A study of the Koran shows **first,** only a limited but yet significant Koranic Surahs have been abrogated. **Second,** the abrogation pertains supposedly to legal and practical matters only and does not apply to matters of ideology, belief and practices. However, a closer look we find that multitudes of Surahs have been abrogated.

Today many Muslims scholars agree that up to 500 Surahs are affected by abrogation. The early <u>Muslims were confused</u> and even <u>Muhammad admitted</u> <u>that the Koran was confusing</u>. Challenge your next Muslim

44

contact with this fact and watch him start trying to change or cease the conversation.

Bukhari 6:70 Narrated Aisha "Allah's Apostle recited the verse it is he who has sent down to you the book. In it are verses that are entirely clear, they are the foundation of the book, others not entirely clear. So, as for those in whose hearts there is a deviation (from the truth), follow thereof that is not entirely clear seeking affliction and searching for its hidden meanings; but no one knows its hidden meanings but Allah. And those who are firmly grounded in knowledge say: 'We believe in it (i.e. the Koran) the whole of it (i.e., it's clear and unclear verses) are from our Lord.' And none receive admonition except men of understanding."

Surah 3:7 "It is he who has sent down to you (Muhammad) the Book (this Koran). In it are verses that are entirely clear, they are the foundations of the Book [and those are the verses of commandments, obligatory duties and legal laws for the punishment of thieves and adulterers]; and others not entirely clear. So, as for those in whose hearts there is a deviation (from the truth), they follow that which is not entirely clear thereof seeking (polytheism and trials) and seeking for its hidden meanings; but none know its hidden meanings save Allah. And those who are firmly grounded in knowledge say. We believe in it (the Koran) the whole of it

(clear and unclear verses) are from our Lord.
And none receive admonition except men of
understanding."

But many Muslims claim that there are no Koranic
Surahs that abrogate other Koranic Surahs, but that the Koran
only abrogates other scriptures. This position is untenable.
Muhammad himself believed that <u>some Surahs were
cancelled or removed</u> and that the early Muslims understood
abrogation explicitly as a Koranic Surah replacing or
canceling another.

The Koran Supports Abrogation

Here are actual Koranic Surahs that reference
abrogation.

Surah 2:106 "If we abrogate a verse or cause it to
be forgotten, we will replace it by a better
one or one similar..."

Surah 13:39 "Allah blots out what he wills and
confirms (what he wills). And with him is
the Mother of the Book."

Surah 17:86 "If we willed we could surely take
away that which we have revealed to you
(i.e. this Koran). Then you would find no
protector against us in that respect."

Surah 16:101 "When we change a verse (of the
Koran) in place of another and Allah knows
best what he sends down...they say you
(Muhammad) are a forger, liar...."

Surah 22:52 "Never did we send a messenger or a
prophet before you but when he did <u>recite</u>

the revelation or narrated or spoke (Satan) threw (some falsehood) in it. But Allah abolishes that which Satan throws in. Then Allah establishes his own revelations."

This last Surah is connected to what are known as the Satanic Surahs. Very early, Muhammad compromised with paganism to gain support and uttered a Koranic revelation allowing idol worship. Later, he said that Allah showed him he had been tricked by Satan and spoke Satan's words. His revelation allowing idol worship was then removed from the recital of the Koran, and another put in its place.

The abrogation of the Koran is not only with the Koran itself, but also the Koran toward earlier revelations such as those given by Moses (the Koran is not organized chronologically). There has been a whole subset of theological scholarship, (research) and study to ascertain which Surahs abrogate and which are abrogated. There is a list of some abrogating/abrogated Koranic Surahs and there are many cases of abrogation, however, we will look at only a few examples.

Koranic Subjects Abrogated

Surah 2:142-144: concerning the direction of prayer. We find the change of the (Qibla) direction of prayer from Jerusalem to Mecca. **Surah 4:15: The change of punishment for adultery.** It is seen as either an example of abrogation of the Koran by the Sunni, or as an example of a

Surah that stresses life imprisonment (accruing to what was then changed to 100 strokes by flogging according to **Surah 24:2).** Yet Islamic law prescribes stoning, based on the practice of Muhammad, who commanded to stone those guilty of adultery. The punishment of stoning for adultery is seen as an example of a Surah of which the reading has been abrogated (removed from the text of the Koran) but the meaning remains in force. On the other hand, **Surah 4:15 and 24:2** are abrogated in meaning, while the text remains in the Koran for recitation. Today Muslims stone to death or cut the heads off hundreds of women every year for adultery, even if the woman was raped by her brother, father or a stranger. Remember in Islam, women are treated as property, they have no rights. There are no human rights in Islam.

Islam-The Fighting Ability and Victory

The fighting ability of victory for Muslims is also abrogated by one verse following the next.

Surah 8:65-66 "O Prophet, urge the believers to fight. If there are twenty steadfast persons amongst you, they will overcome two hundred, and if there be a hundred steadfast persons, they will overcome a thousand of those who disbelieve (non-Muslims), because they (disbelievers) are people who do not understand.(**66**) Now Allah has now lightened your (task), for he knows there is weakness in you. So if there are a thousand of you, they shall overcome two thousand with the leave of Allah. And Allah is with (the patient)."

Jihad (The Sword)

The sword Surahs, "the call to fight and slay the pagan (non-Muslim) wherever you find them," **(Surah 9:5)** or "strike off their heads in battle," **(Surah 47:5)** or "make war on the unbeliever (non-Muslim) in Allah, until they pay tribute," **(Surah 9:29)** or "until the religion be all of it Allah's," **(Surah 8:39)** or "a grievous penalty against those who reject the Islamic faith," **(Surah 9:3)** contradict that "there is to be no compulsion in religion" **(Surah 2:256)**. **Note here that Surah 9 was one of the last Surahs to be revealed to Muhammad.** Logically, it abrogates the Surah that says there is no compulsion in Islam.

The Night Prayer Reduced

The night prayer performed by reciting the Koran ought to be more or less half the time of the night **(Surah 73:20)**. This was changed to, as much as may be easy for you **(Surah 20)**.

The Money Inherited by Wife

In Surah 2:240 if the husband dies, the wife can have his money before she marries another person, but in **(Surah 2:234)** she must be in mourning, then 4 months and 10 days after her husband dies, she can marry another man.

Christians and Jews Rewarded

In **Surah 2:62 and 5:69** says Jews and Christians will have a reward from Allah, but in **Surah 3:85,** and **Surah 4:89** say that anyone who will follow or seek a religion other than Islam will never be accepted by Allah.

Drinking Wine (Unclean)

Surah 2:219 and 5:90 drinking wine and sex are unclean things, but in **Surah 4:43,** it states that wine may be drank. As to sex, Islamic men find liberty in following Muhammad's immoral, salacious, sexual lifestyle, thus multiple wives, and divorce of his wife just by saying, "I divorce you" three times.

Fighting with Christians

Both **Surahs 2:109 and 60:8-9** say "don't fight with the people of the book or religion," but it is abrogated by **Surah 9:29,** which says "**fight them until they believe in Allah and make them pay tax.**" Any Muslim who reads, listens to or in any way believes the Koran will seek to subdue by conversion or killing of every non-Muslim.

Allah's Message or Satanic Message?

Surah 53:11-12 it was Allah's message and in **Surah 22:52** it became Satan's message which means Satan gave some revelations to Muhammad.

Illegal sex (Adultery)

In **Surah 4:15-17:** "If any person committed adultery or illegal sex, if people testify against him and if he will take the woman as his wife, their sin is forgiven." **But Surah 24:2** says: "if any unmarried person committed adultery or illegal sex he will be punished with 100 stripes but if he is a married man he will be stoned to death." It must be realized that in most, if not all Islam today, the man is not stoned or even put in prison for extramarital sex. Muslim men are allowed to take multiple wives. In fact, they are permitted to have temporary wives, up to three nights then let them go (divorce them). This practice allows the immoral extra-marital sex in a manner approved by Islam.

Marriage of Muhammad

In **Surah 33:6** Allah stopped him from marrying other women, but in **Surah 33:50** he (Muhammad) can marry any time and from any house that is his privilege as a prophet; not for all Muslims. Muhammad would take wives away from his most trusted male supporters and followers claiming Allah told him to do so. Muhammad had fourteen wives, one only six years of age. Because of his marriage to a six year old girl, Muhammad can legitimately be called "**a pedophile**."

The Payment of Prophet

Surah 58:12 there is payment for the prophet for consultation in private. If somebody needs to meet with him, he must pay first, but in **Surah 58:13** that payment will be changed to pray or to give a gift for the poor.

The Fear of Allah

Surah 3:102 "Fear of Allah and obeying his command is a must," but **Surah 64:16** says "fear Allah as much as you can it is not an obligation."

Abrogation from the Hadith of Bukhara

In **Bukhari's Hadith** collection, there contains a number of examples of abrogation. These also illustrate the confusion from the earliest days of Islam concerning abrogation.

Bukhari 6:32   Narrated Ata that he heard Ibn Abbas reciting the Divine verse--"And for those who can fast they had a choice either fast or feed the poor for ever day **(Surah 2:184)** Ibn Abbas said this verse is not abrogated, but it is meant for old men and old women who have no strength to fast, so they should feed one poor person for each day of fasting (instead of fasting).

Bukhari 6:34   Narrated Salama when the Divine Revelation--"for these who can fast they had a choice either fast or feed a poor for every day."

When **Surah 2:184** was revealed, it was permissible for one to give a ransom and give up fasting until the Surah succeeding it was revealed and abrogated.

Bukhari 6:53 Narrated Ibn Az-Zubair "I said to Uthman bin Affan (while he was collecting the Koran) regarding the verse--those of you who died and leave wives...**Surah 2:240,** this verse was abrogated by another verse so why should you write it or leave it in the Koran? Uthman said o son of my brother, I will not shift anything of it from its place."

Bukhari 6:69 Narrated Marwan Al-Asghar: "A man from the companions of Allah's Apostle who, I think, was Ibn Umar said, the verse whether you show what is in your minds or conceal it was abrogated by the verse following it."

Bukhari 6:285 Narrated Al- Qasim bin Abi Bazza "That he asked Said bin Jubair, is there any repentance of the one who has murdered a believer intentionally? Then I recited to him; nor kill such life as Allah has forbidden except for a just cause. Said said, I recited this very verse before Ibn Abbas as you have recited it before me. Ibn Abbas said this verse was revealed in Mecca and it has been abrogated by a verse in surah an-Nisa which was later revealed in Medina.

Ala bal- shikhkir said, "The messenger of **Allah abrogated some of his commands** by others, just as the Koran abrogates some part with the other." It's clear that the companions of Muhammad were taught the concept of abrogation from Muhammad, for they uniformly applied it in the same manner with <u>one Surah canceling out another.</u> In these examples, there are no references to other scriptures or other religions, but rather it is central to Islam. During Muhammad's final year, <u>he supposedly had the Koran recited to him twice by Gabriel and then reviewed the changes</u> with ibn Masud, there were enough crucial changes made that the last year, Muhammad needed to teach them to his top Koranic disciple ibn Masud.

The Koran Fixed and Unchanging?

Surah 4:82 "Do they not consider the Koran had it been from other than Allah they would surely have found therein much discrepancies."

Surah 10:64 "No change can there be in the words of Allah…"

<u>Yet it abrogates and changes itself from the very beginning until now,</u> people have seen through Muhammad's claims and found multitudes of discrepancies, deceptions and lies. Indeed the words and message are from demon spirits." The source materials prove that the traditional doctrine of abrogation is the correct one, i e. the Koran is an abrogation in itself. **The Koran is simply a compilation of sayings, musings and perversions of what Muhammad and his followers knew or heard of Holy Scriptures, both the Bible and the Torah. Muhammad rejected the Jews and Christians and**

decided to develop an ideology for his actions and secure followers himself.

The Argument that Abrogation does not Affect the Koran is Deceitful.

Some of the abrogation may not seem to be very serious contradictions, but the Koran claims to be the pure, authentic words of Allah. Therefore, changes, deletions or abrogation show Allah to be vacillating, changing and unsure; whereas the God of the Bible is the same yesterday, today and forever. This simply proves that the (considered to be) original, uncreated, preserved tablets in heaven from which the Koran came are really impure, inaccurate and changing. The Koran is a demonic book.

A sentence in the main prayer for all Muslims from the al-Buruj preceded (**Surah 85:22**) implies the abrogation that the root is corrupt. When the Koran came from Heaven it was perfect, but has not remained pure since then. The doctrine of abrogation presents Allah as capricious, erratic and changeable, and it casts Muhammad in a doubtful light. **This god (Allah) couldn't make up his mind and because of his confusion, Muslims today are uncertain (privately) about what rules are applicable in their own religion.** Someone said Muhammad is like Felix the cat... Whenever he gets in a fix, he reaches into his bag of tricks to get out of a jam or change the way he wanted things done.

The abrogations shaped Islam over Muhammad's 23 years of <u>claimed prophet-hood</u>. **As Muhammad grew in power, Islam changed from peaceful to violent.** The history of Islam is two stages, one, <u>the peaceful stage</u> until strength in numbers, and two, <u>the warring stage</u> when there are enough followers. If it is true that the measure of a man is what he does with power, then <u>Muhammad proved himself to be a very small, evil, wicked, violent, immoral man</u>, for he used his power to subject people brutally and compel them to accept Islam or be killed. **The trail of blood behind Muhammad grew ever wider, and through terrorism, murder and brutality continues globally today.** In the book, "**<u>Islam, Evil in the name of god</u>,**"says 270,000,000 have been murdered by Islam, thus the greatest holocaust in history. Wake up America; look at the Netherlands, Africa, Europe, France, Germany, Russia, London, the U.K. We see it today in Egypt, Iran, Libya, Syria and most Muslim countries.

The Koran's god is **not the true God.** Muslims who have put their faith in Muhammad and the Koran will one day**, to their horror,** see that **they have been duped and sent into everlasting hell,** without redemption and no hope for all of eternity.

4

$\mathscr{I}$slam and **THE HOLY BIBLE**

The Koran's View of The Bible

The Koran is presented as the foremost, final, infallible witness of Allah and alleges that the Bible is not accurate or complete thus needing the Koran to complete the revelation. Islam contends that God's word, The Holy Bible, is corrupt, flawed, inaccurate and without final authority or trustworthiness.

The Bible; a book for Muslim teaching, but not divine.

Surah 2:136 "Say O Muslims! We believe in Allah and that which has been sent down to us, that which has been sent down to Abraham, Ishmael, Isaac, Jacob and the tribes, and that given to Moses, Jesus, and given to the prophets from their Lord. We make no distinction between any of them..."

Islam views the Bible as given by Allah to Moses and to Jesus, all viewed as prophets of Allah. The Law of Moses and the Gospel of Jesus are only guides to mankind. The belief that Allah sent the Old and New Testaments as a precursor to the Koran is clearly seen in the third Surah.

Surah 3:2-3 "Allah! None has the right to be worshipped but he…It is he who has sent down the Book (Koran) to you (Muhammad) with truth, confirming what came before it. He sent down the Torah and the Gospel."

Surah 5:44, 46, 47, 48 "Verily we did send down the Torah (to Moses); therein was guidance and light…and if whosoever does not judge by what Allah has revealed they are no better than disbelievers...We sent Jesus, the son of Mary, confirming the Torah that had come before him, we gave him the gospel in which was guidance and light…a guidance and an admonition for the pious...Let the people of the gospel judge by what Allah has revealed herein. And whosoever does not judge by what Allah has revealed, (then) such (people) are the rebellious, disobedient (of a lesser degree) to Allah."

The third Surah is confirmed by three additional interesting texts.

Surah 5:68 "O People of the Scripture...act according to the Torah, the gospel, and what has now come down to you from your Lord…"

Surah 10:37 "The Koran is a confirmation of (the revelation) which was before it..."

Surah 10:94 "So if you were in doubt (Muhammad) concerning that which we have revealed unto you then ask these who have been reading the Book before you. The truth has come to you from your Lord."

Muslims are commanded not to argue with the Jew or Christian over the revelation, but to emphasize that Allah has added the Koran to the divine revelation, <u>to correct the words of the Holy Bible</u>. It is not unlike the claim of Mormonism, that the book of Mormon is the final revelation, thus taking precedence over the Bible.

Surah 29:46 "And argue not with the people of the Scripture (Jews and Christians), unless it be in (a way) that is better (with good words and good manner, inviting them to Islamic Monotheism)...say (to them) We believe in that which has been revealed to us and revealed to you...."

This Surah proves a very important point; Muslims see the Koran not as contradicting the Old and New Testaments but as fulfilling them, thus, <u>the final authority</u>. The Jew and Christian are called to testify to this truth and validate Islam according to Islamic teaching.

Surah 21:7 "And we sent not before you (O Muhammad) but men to whom we revealed. So ask the people of the [Scriptures, Torah, Gospel] Remember if you do not know."

The Old and New Testaments are seen to be divinely given but humanly corrupted. The Jew and the Christian are called by the Koran to recognize that the Bible was corrupted by lies and distortions from Christians and Jews, therefore, without final authority, and the Koran is pure, perfect and without flaw.

Surah 3:71 "O people of the Scripture (Jews and Christians) why do you mix truth with falsehood and conceal the truth while you know?"

Surah 3:78 "And verily among them is a party who distort the Book with their tongues (As they read) so that you may think it is from the Book, but this is not from the book…"

The Koran and the Bible Conflicts

A major amount of the teachings in the Koran directly contradicts the Bible. These contradictions draw attention to discrepancies of theology and thought between the Muslims and Christians, as any attempt to witness to them will fail. Since Islam teaches that the Bible has been corrupted, thus the Muslims believe their version of the Biblical narratives of the Biblical stories given to Muhammad to correct the corrupted; they view their versions of the Biblical narratives to be the only ones correct. A number of Surahs teach that Allah sent the revisions of the Biblical stories to Muhammad to fix the corrupted Bible.

Surah 6:34 "Verily (many) messengers were denied before you, (o Muhammad), but with patience they bore the denial, and they were hurt; till our help reached them, and none can alter the words (decisions) of Allah. Surely there has reached you the information (news) about the messengers (before you)."

Surah 4:82 "Do they not then consider the Koran carefully? Had it been from other than Allah, they would have surely found therein many a contradiction."

Surah 10:65 "And let not their speech grieve you (o Muhammad), for all power and honor belong to Allah."

Examples of Koranic Deception

Moses' Adoption

According to the Koran:

Surah 28:9 "Pharaoh's wife adopted Moses."

According to the Bible:

Exodus 2:10 states that "Pharaoh's daughter adopted Moses.."

But, the Koran says that it was his wife. However, if Pharaoh's wife adopted Moses, he would then be the son of Pharaoh himself and heir to the throne of Egypt.

The Trinity

According to the Koran:

Surah 5:116 "Christians worship three gods: the father, the mother-Mary, and the son Jesus."

Surah 5:73-75 "Surely disbelievers are those who said Allah is the third of the three (in a Trinity).."

Obviously, the accusation is against Christians and is an erroneous assumption that the trinity makes God one of three, including Mary, the mother of Jesus. Needles to say, Islam completely rejects the Trinity.

According to the Bible:

The trinity consists of three; the Father, Son and the Holy Spirit, all co-equal and have the same attributes, yet only one God. It is the tri-unity of the God-Head. According to **Colossians 2:9**, Jesus is the fullness of the God-Head bodily. Jesus is God!

Pharaoh and the Tower of Babel

According to the Koran:

Surah 28:38 Says that a man named Haman, a servant of Pharaoh, was ordered to built a high tower to ascend to God.

According to the Bible:

The tower of Babel is found in Genesis chapter 11, long before there were Pharaohs, and the name Haman is a much later name in scripture. The only Haman in scripture is in the story of Esther in Babylon, which is long after the zenith of Egypt's glory.

Who built the Israelite calf?

According to the Koran:

Says that the calf worshiped by the Israelites at Mount Horeb was molded by a Samaritan.

According to the Bible:

The term Samaritan did not come into existence until 722 B.C. several hundred years after the exodus when the idol was crafted.

The sacrifice of Abraham's son

According to the Koran:

Surahs 37:100-111: state that Abraham sacrificed his son Ishmael instead of Isaac. This can be supported only by Islamic tradition and marks one of the two holidays of Islam.

According to the Bible:

The Hebrew text of the Old Testament, Genesis chapter 22, identify the son of Abraham who was laid upon the altar for sacrifice. The context says that it was Isaac, yet **Surah 37 identifies Ishmael.**

Who led Gideon's army?

According to the Koran:

Surah 2:247 makes Saul the general of this army although the king was not yet born.

According to the Bible:

Judges 7 identifies Gideon as the leader of the three-hundred man army of soldiers chosen by God.

Jesus' Crucifixion

According to the Koran:

Surah 4:157 "And because of their saying in boast (the Jews) we killed Messiah (Christ) Jesus the son of Mary the messenger of Allah; but they killed him not, nor crucified him, but it appeared so to them."

According to the Bible:

Jesus was indeed crucified. The parallel Gospels all verify Jesus' crucifixion and many other Old Testament and New Testament text point to or refer to the crucifixion of Jesus.

We can simply say that the Koran is a deceitful compilation of sayings that Muhammad himself said came from demonic voices speaking to him. Much of the Koran was developed long after the life of Muhammad and is **not divinely** inspired. The entire Koran is a deceitful, demonic book that deludes and dooms billions. Yet, we can place full trust and total confidence in every word of the Bible as real, genuine, trustworthy and accurate; without error, inspired of Holy God.

Because Muslims trust and believe the commands of a demonic book (the Koran), they are ready to kill all non-Muslims who refuse to submit to Allah.

THE KEY DETERMINATION FOR THE MUSLIM IS, "IF YOU ARE COMFORTABLE IN YOUR HEART, DECEIT AND LIES ARE ACCEPTABLE."

5

$\mathscr{Islam}$ and **DECEPTION**

Muslims believe that war, either political, social or military authorizes deception, therefore, **lying is a fundamental element in Islam**. Muslims are commanded to purposefully hide what they truly believe in order to mislead non-Muslims. The true nature of their religion in other words, it's ok to lie to non-Muslims to shroud the real truth in order to prevail on an issue. An example of this is Dr. Parvez Ahmed, the National director of C.A.I.R. from 2003-2008. Ahmed was being questioned by the Jacksonville, Florida City Council in view of an appointment to the Jacksonville Human Rights Commission. He was asked if he would defend the Constitution, he replied "yes." When, in reality, a Muslim cannot have loyalty to the Constitution of the United States, as his real loyalty is to the Koran; which is against everything the Constitution represents.

The morality of lying is one of the most complex aspects of Islamic thought. As a result, it creates theimpression that whether a person is truthful, or deceitful, depends entirely on the situation. A Muslim will tell you one thing while knowing that the complete opposite is in fact the truth. This is very much like what is called situation ethics, lying to prevail or protect the real truth or position of the person telling the lie.

There Are Three Categories of Lies

A lie against Allah is not permitted in Islam

Surah 6:93 "who can be more unjust than he who invents a lie against Allah or says a revelation has come to me whereas no revelation has come to him in anything, and who says I will reveal that like of what Allah has revealed. And if you could but see when the (polytheists and wrongdoers are in the agonies of death, while the angels are stretching forth their hands (saying) Deliver your souls! This day you shall be recompensed with the torment of degradation because of what you used to utter against Allah other than the truth. And you used to reject his (proofs, evidences, verses, lessons, signs, revelations, etc.) with disrespect!"

A lie against Muhammad not permitted

Bukhara 2:378 narrated Al-Mughira: "I heard the prophet saying, ascribing false things to me is not like ascribing false things to anyone else. Whosoever tells lie against me intentionally then surely let him occupy his seat in Hell-Fire."

Lying and deception are permitted in Islam

Bukhari 3:857 "Humid bin Abdu- al Rah man bin Auf reported that his mother Umm Kulthum bint Uqba heard Allah's messenger as saying, a liar is not one who tries to bring reconciliation amongst people and speaks good in order to avert dispute, or he conveys good." Ibn' Shihab said he did not hear that exemption was granted in anything that speaks a lie in three cases: in battle, for bringing reconciliation amongst persons (the narration of the words of the husband to his wife and the narration of the words of a wife to her husband is twisted from in order to bring reconciliation between them)."

History reveals that this was clear in Muhammad's life and his teaching in Mecca and after. Muhammad was the peaceful, harmless lamb in Mecca, but in Medina he became a vicious, warring, roaring lion. Muslims will give a peace talk or peace agreement to buy favor or time while they make other plans for favor, control or bringing the non-Muslims to submission. The two stages of Islam are peace and war. Peace until Muslims become large enough and powerful enough to overthrow the government they live under. Then sharia law is instituted.

Muhammad's Attitude About Lying

Muhammad treated truth and deception according to his own style of situational ethics. Muhammad

condoned, and actually permitted, lying to achieve his goals, and the ultimate goal of Islam.

Bukhara 5:369 narrated Jabir bin Abdullah Allah Apostle said, "who is willing to kill ka'b bin Al-Ashraf who has hurt Allah and his Apostle?" Thereupon Muhammad bin Maslama got up saying 'o Allah's Apostle, would you like that I will kill him? The prophet said 'yes.' Muhammad bin Maslama said, 'allow me to say a false thing to deceive ka'b," the prophet said, 'you may say it' ...."

Muhammad's First Allowance for Lying

The first time that the prophet Muhammad permitted denying Islam or denying him as a prophet was with Amar Ben Yasser who was one of Muhammad's friends, was captured and held hostage by the tribe of Quraish. The tribe tortured Yasser, so he denied Muhammad and Islam to gain freedom. After they set him free, he went back to Muhammad and confessed what had taken place. Muhammad told Yasser if that ever happened to him again he should do exactly what he did with no shame, thus authorizing deceit, lying for the cause of Allah.

Al-Bayaqi 16:106 Narrated by Abd al-Razak, Ibn Sa'd, Ibn Jarir, Ibn Abi Hatim, Ibn Mardawayh, al-Bayhaqi in his book, "Al-Dala-il," and it was corrected by al-Hakim in his book "al-Mustadrak" that "the non believers arrested Ammar Ibn Yasirr (RA) and (tortured him until) he (RA) uttered foul word's about the prophet (PBUH & HF) and praised their gods (idols) and when they released him, (RA) he (RA) went straight to the prophet (PBUH & HF). The prophet said, 'is there something on your mind?' Ammar Ibn Yasir said 'bad news, they would not release me until I defamed you (PBUH & HF) and praised their gods. The prophet said 'how you find your heart to be?' Ammar answered 'comfortable with faith', so the prophet said then if they come back for you then do the same thing all over again."

Then the key determination for the Muslim is, "if you are comfortable in your heart," the deceit and lies are acceptable.

Allah's Revelation to Muhammad

Surah 16:106 "Whoever disbelieved in Allah after his belief, except him who is forced thereto and whose heart is at rest with faith but such as open their breasts to disbelief, on them is wrath from Allah and theirs will be a great torment."

So, Muhammad actually authorized Muslims to lie, blaspheme and deny their belief if it was going to protect them as long as they were comfortable in the heart. The Koran also commands not to be friends or helpers to non-Muslims.

71

Surah 3:28 "Let not the believers (Muslims) take the disbelievers (non-Muslims) as (supporters, helpers) instead of the believers (Muslims), and whoever does that will never be helped by Allah in any way, except if you indeed fear a danger from them. And Allah warns you against himself (his punishment) and to Allah is the final return."

In conclusion, <u>a Muslim will, and with the authority of the Koran, lie</u> to bring about his desired answer or result in any situation, even if it means danger or destruction for society or a nation. The only goal for Islam is to ultimately gain global, universal control. Never trust a Muslim to speak the truth when he is in a debate, dialogue or discussion regarding the issues of Islam.

6

Islam and MUHAMMAD
The Sinner

Islam says and believes that Muhammad was not a sinner, but when we look at the sinner in Islam, we must look at the life and the teaching of Muhammad. It is known that all Muslims follow Muhammad's teaching as found in the Koran and his life story in the Hadith. When we examine the prayers expressed by Muhammad, we can understand the depth of sin he knew was in his life. It acknowledges a nature within that is bent towards sin, and it reflects the desire to cleanse that depth of sin. We hear in his prayer a man's struggle with sin. He asks Allah's forgiveness (but Allah can't) for his past and future sins, because he knows that as a normal man, he is going to sin, it is inevitable. He asks Allah for forgiveness for things he has done intentionally, and unintentionally. He knows that the sins he has committed are evil and confesses that to Allah. He does not make light of his sins. He realizes that his sins are filthy in God's eyes. However, he confesses his sins to a false god-Allah.

The prayer was prayed by Muhammad and it is a synthesis of his personal prayers found in Sahih Bukhara. We find evidence in both the Hadith and the Koran that **Muhammad was a sinner, and that he knew he was. Yet, Islamic teaching is that Muhammad is some sinless deity.**

The Evidence in the Hadith

Bukhari 8:335 Narrated by Shaded bin Aus the prophet said "the most superior way of asking for forgiveness from Allah, "I acknowledge and confess you, please as no one can forgive sins except you. Forgive my mistakes , those done intentionally, or out of my ignorance, with or without seriousness, oh Allah forgive my sin and my ignorance, forgive my sins of the future, which I did openly or secretly, forgive the wrong I have done jokingly or seriously. I seek your protection from all the evil I have done. Wash away my sins, and cleanse my heart from all the sins as a white garment is from the filth, and let there be long distance between me and my sins, as you made the east and west far from each other."

Bukhari 8:379 Narrated by Aisha the prophet used it, "o Allah I seek refuge with you from laziness and geriatric old age from all kinds of sins and from being in debt from the affliction of the fire and from the punishment of the fire and from the evil of the affliction of wealth: and I seek refuge with you from the affliction of poverty, and I seek refuge with you from the affliction of

Al-Masih Ad dajjal. O Allah washes away my sins with the water of snow and hail and cleanses my heart from all the sins as with garments cleansed from the filth, and let there be a long distance between me and my sins, as you made east and west far from each other."

Bukhari 8:407 Narrated by Abu muses Muhammad used to invoke Allah with the following invocation. "O my Lord forgive my sins and my ignorance and my exceeding the limits; boundaries of righteousness in all my deeds what you know better than I, o Allah forgive my mistakes, those done intentionally or out of my ignorance or without or with seriousness, and I confess that all such mistakes are done by me o Allah forgive my sins of the past and of the future which I did openly or secretly you are the one who makes the things go before, and you are the one who delays them and you are the omnipotent".

Bukhari 8:408 narrated by Abu- Musa Al-Ash ari, the prophet used to invoke Allah saying "forgive my mistakes and my ignorance and my exceeding the limited boundaries of righteousness, forgive all my deeds and whatever you know better than. Allah forgive the wrong I have done jokingly or seriously, and forgive my accidental and intentional errors, all that is present in me."

Muhammad Knew He Was a Sinner

Thus, he makes his confession public. Over and over again confessing that he was a sinner. In the Koran he admits he is a sinner, yet <u>Muslims today say that Muhammad was not a sinner</u>, they believe that he was pure and perfect. Muhammad was simply a sinful, demonically-controlled Jihadist.

<u>Muslims believe</u> **that Allah gives <u>a special protection</u> to his prophets from being sinners.**

The Evidence in the Koran

Surah 40:55 "So be patient (o Muhammad). Verily, the promise of Allah is true, and ask forgiveness for your fault and glorify the praises of your Lord (in the time period from early morning or sunrise till before midnoon)..."

Surah 47:19 So know (o Muhammad) that (none has the right to be worshipped but Allah) and ask forgiveness for your sin and also for (the sin) of believing men and believing women. And Allah knows well your moving about and your place of rest (in your homes)."

Surah 48:2 "That Allah may forgive you your sins of the past and the future and complete his favor on you, and guide you on the straight path..."

Muhammad's entire life was filled with sins he committed; rape, murder, robbery, theft, immorality, no

wonder he prayed for forgiveness. The fact of sin was deep in his heart and recognition. Yet he did not know the Creator—God of the Holy Bible, or Jesus Christ, who alone can atone for man's sins.

Muhammad admitted he was a sinner and an evil person. However, later Muslims invented a teaching that Muhammad was not a sinner. If Muhammad himself acknowledges his sin and asks for forgiveness, then, all Muslims are sinners; they need forgiveness of sins. Unless forgiven, through Jesus Christ's shed blood on Calvary, all Muslims as has Muhammad will go to hell without hope.

Jesus Christ, God incarnate, is the only man that ever lived who was sinless because He was and is God come in the flesh to shed His blood on the cross as payment for the sins of the whole world. Whosoever will may come to Jesus for forgiveness of sin.

"SAY (O MUHAMMAD) HE IS ALLAH
(THE) ONE, THE SELF SUFFICIENT
MASTER WHOM ALL CREATURES NEED
(HE NEITHER EATS NOR DRINKS) HE
BEGETS NOT NOR WAS HE BEGOTTEN."

SURAH 112:1-3

"HE IS THE ORIGINATOR OF THE
HEAVENS AND THE EARTH. HOW CAN HE
HAVE CHILDREN WHEN HE HAS NO WIFE?
HE CREATED ALL THINGS AND HE IS THE
ALL KNOWER OF EVERYTHING."

SURAH 6:101

7

Islam and **JESUS**

All Muslims **claim** to believe in Jesus. Muslims are quick to demonstrate good will for Jesus and his mother, Mary. The name of Jesus is found 25 times in the Koran. **Islam considers Jesus a prophet just like Moses, Abraham and Noah, <u>but rejects the divinity of Jesus Christ</u>.** Islam completely rejects the Biblical truth that Jesus Christ is God come in the flesh to become the payment for our sins through His death on the cross. But if Jesus is just a man, we are all dead in trespasses and sin.

The chief question to be asked of any religion, cult or spiritual movement is; "<u>Who is Jesus?</u>" Is He fully man and fully God? Anything less is not the Jesus of the Bible. Islam claims to believe in Jesus and is very quick to tell Christians of their benevolent belief in Jesus, yet Islam completely rejects the fact that Jesus is God come in the flesh.

The Koran's Teachings About Jesus

His name and its significance

Christians believe that Jesus is the Greek from Joshua, which means (savior) the Lord saves and occurs in the Holy Bible around twelve hundred times. However in Islam, Jesus is known as "Isa." In the Koran, the name Isa often occurs with the addition "son of Maryam (Mary)." Of the 25 places in the Koran where Isa is used in sixteen of them he is called Ibn Maryam (the son of Mary), and in five passages his name is coupled with that of Moses. Remember the Koran has no chronological order.

The Koran does not mention who chose the name and why he was named Isa. The Bible tells us the name Jesus was chosen by God himself, **"You shall call His name 'Jesus' for He shall save His people from their sins."** (Matt. 1:21)

Surah 2:87 "we gave Jesus the son of Mary clear signs and supported him with Gabriel..."

Surah 5:46 "and in their footsteps we sent Jesus the son of Mary; confirming the Torah that had come before Him, and we gave Him the gospel in which was guidance and light..."

Surah 4:171 "The Messiah Jesus the son of Mary was **no more than a messenger of Allah's and his word...which he bestowed on Mary...say not three (Trinity)! For Allah is but one God."**

Surah 5:116 "Allah will say Jesus the son of Mary did you ever say to worship me and my mother as God beside Allah?"

The Koran acknowledges that **Jesus was born without a father**. Mary, his mother was chosen by Allah for this purpose. The Koran highly reveres her. **Surah 19** of the Koran is given her name. **The Koran completely rejects the divinity of Jesus Christ with absoluteness**.

The Miraculous Birth of Jesus

Surah 3:42 "And (remember) when the angels said O Mary! Verily, Allah has chosen you, purified you (from polytheism and disbelief) and chosen you above the women of (mankind and jinn) (of her life time)."

Surah 21:91 "And she who guarded her chastity [Virgin Mary] we breathed into (the sleeves of) her (shirt or garment) through our Gabriel and we made her and her son [Jesus] a sign for all (the mankind and jinn)."

Surah 66:12 "And Mary, the daughter of Imran who guarded her chastity. And we breathed into (the sleeve of her or her shirt or her garment) through our spirit (Gabriel) and she testified to the truth of the words of her Lord (i.e. believed the words of Allah (be; and he was) that is **Jesus son of Mary as a messenger of Allah** and (also believed in) his scriptures and she was of (the obedient to Allah)."

Surah 23:50 "And we made the son of Mary and his mother as a sign, and we gave them refuge on high ground, a place of rest, security and flowing streams."

Born of a Virgin

In line with other Koran references, the designated son of Mary is given to remind readers that Jesus was born of the Virgin Mary. She conceived Jesus through Allah's creative word. However, the virgin birth in the Koran is vastly different and foreign to the Biblical record. It is evident, the Koran text indicates that Islam has no concept of what "virgin birth" connotes.

Surah 3:47 She said "o my Lord how shall I have a son when no man has touched me? He said so (it will be) for Allah creates what he wills. When he has decreed something he says to it only 'be'- and it is."

Bukhari 4:506 "Muhammad said when any human being is born, Satan touches him at both sides of the body with his two fingers except Jesus, the son of Mary, whom Satan tried to touch but failed, for he touched the placenta cover instead."

Jesus Instructs to Worship Allah

Jesus is called by his proper name along with the title Al-Messiah. This title is sometimes accompanied by Jesus and sometimes used by itself and **occurs in the Koran some eleven times**. This title is used in a personal way.

Surah 5:72 "Surely they have disbelieved who say 'Allah is the Messiah Isa son of Mary.' But the Messiah <u>Isa said 'o children of Israel!</u> <u>Worship Allah, my Lord</u> and your Lord. Verily whosoever sets up partners (in worship) with Allah then has forbidden paradise to him and the fire will be his abode. And for the polytheists (Christians) and wrong doers there are no helpers."

Islam says that <u>if Jesus claims to be God, Allah will send Him (Jesus) to Hell.</u>

Blessed by Allah

However Muslim commentators and scholars give various explanations and the Koran says that Jesus was blessed by Allah.

Surah 19:31-32 "And he (Allah) has made me blessed where ever I be and has enjoined on me prayer and Zakat as long as I live. And dutiful to my mother, and made me not arrogant, unblest."

Anointed at Birth

And so anointed with honor, He had been protected from Satan from his birth. The encyclopedia of Islam attaches this special anointing to his birth.

Surah 3:36 "Then when she gave birth to her child [Mary], she said: o my Lord I have given birth to a female child –and Allah knew better what she brought forth— and the male is not like the female and I have named her (Mary), and I seek refuge with you (Allah) for her and for her offspring from Satan the outcast."

Islam Rejects Jesus' Son-ship

The Koran denies that **Allah begets or takes to himself offspring in several places in the Koran**. Allah has no son! God does; His name is Jesus Christ!

Surah 112:1-3 "say (o Muhammad) he is Allah (the) one, the Self Sufficient Master whom all creatures need (he neither eats nor drinks) **he begets not nor** was he begotten."

Surah 6:101 "He is the originator of the heavens and the earth. **How can he have** children when He has no wife? He created all things and he is the all knower of everything."

Surah72:3 "And He, exalted be the majesty of our Lord, has **taken neither a wife nor a son (or offspring or children)."**

Therefore if Allah has no son, and the Bible teaches that God had a son, then this is Koranic proof that Allah and God are not the same.

Denies the Trinity

Muslims use these passages which condemn the doctrine of the son-ship of Christ as we know from Scripture. It is also true that the Koran denies the doctrine of the Trinity.

Surah 4:171 "O people of the Scripture (Christians)! Do not exceed the limits in your religion, nor say of Allah aught but the truth. <u>The Messiah (Jesus) son of Mary was</u> <u>(no more than) a messenger of Allah</u> and his word 'be— and was' which he bestowed on Mary and a spirit created by him, so believe in Allah and his messengers. <u>**Say not three**</u> <u>**(Trinity)! Cease! (it is) better for you.**</u> <u>**For Allah is (the only) one, glory be to**</u> <u>**him (Far exalted is he) above having a**</u> <u>**son**</u>. To him belongs all that is in the heavens and all that is in the earth. And Allah is all sufficient as a disposer of affairs."

However, what Islam denies is the Trinity of the Father, Mother and Son, (which Muhammad thought was the doctrine of the trinity) this was due to the Catholic emphasis on Mary, which was Muhammad's view of Christianity.

Surah 5:116 "And (remember) when Allah will say (on of the Day of Resurrection) O Isa (Jesus) son of Mary! Did you say unto men 'worship me and my mother as two gods besides Allah?' He will say 'glory be to you it was not for me to say what I had no right (to say).' Had I said such a thing, you would surely have known it. You know what is in my inner self though I do not know what you are in yours truly only you are the all knower of all that is hidden (and unseen)."

But nowhere does the Bible suggest that type of Trinity or nothing in the Bible which could suggest that Jesus ever spoke of Mary being taken as a god.

The Miracles of Jesus in Islam

The Koran reports that Jesus performed a series of miracles, such as giving life to birds made of clay by breathing into them, or feeding people from meager supplies were to show that Allah can perform anything without being subject to normal causes. This sounds like some of the text from the Apocrypha.

Surah 5:112 "(Remember) when the disciples said 'O Jesus son of Mary! Can your Lord send down to us a table spread (with food) from heaven? Isa said fear Allah if you are indeed believers."

Surah 5:114 "Isa (Jesus) son of Mary said O Allah our Lord! Send us from heaven a table spread (with food) that there may be for us for the first and the last for us a festival and a sign from you; and provide us with sustenance, for you are the best of sustainers."

In another Surah the Koran mentions Jesus as giving life, but no details are given.

Jesus Foretold the Coming of Muhammad

Muslims believe that one of the most important features of Jesus' mission was to give the **glad tidings of the coming of the prophet Muhammad**. According to the Koran, Jesus gave them the good news of Ahmed (Muhammad) the last messenger of Allah.

Surah 61:6 "And (remember) when Isa (Jesus) son of Mary said O children of Israel! I am the messenger of Allah unto you confirming the Taurat [(Torah) which came] before me, and giving glad tidings of a messenger to come after me whose name shall be Ahmad but when he (Ahmad, i.e. Muhammad) came to them with clear proofs, they said this is plain magic."

It is interesting to know that the Koran also gives the name as Ahmad (Muhammad) for the Holy Spirit.

Jesus' Second Coming in Islam

The mission of Jesus according to Islam is in <u>two phases</u>. The first as a prophet to Israel, the second will be at His second coming when He as a follower of Muhammad, will fight the anti-Christ, and help Muslims to convert the world into Islamic global control. And there are two Surahs in the Koran that Muslims believe indicate the second coming of Jesus:

Surah 4:159 "And there is none of the people of the Scripture (Jews and Christians) but must believe in him [Isa (Jesus) son of Mary as <u>only a messenger of Allah</u> and a human being] before his [Jesus or a Jew or a Christian's] death (at the time of the appearance of the angel of death). And on the day of resurrection, he, Jesus, will be a witness against them."

Surah 43:61 "And he [Jesus son of Mary] shall be a known sign for (the coming of) the Hour (Day of Resurrection) [i.e. Jesus' descent on the earth]. Therefore have no doubt concerning it (i.e. the Day of Resurrection). And follow me (Allah) (i.e. be obedient to Allah and do what he orders you to do O mankind)! This is the straight path (of Islamic monotheism leading to Allah and to His paradise)."

According to the first Surah, <u>all the Jews and Christians will believe in Jesus before his death.</u> Muslim commentators must believe this refers to an event in the future. This they believe could only be possible should <u>Jesus come again and live in this world till he dies.</u> The second Surah shows that Jesus is the sign of the last hour. Those Muslims who do believe Jesus will come again; **see Him in a subordinate role to that of the prophet Muhammad of Islam. <u>Jesus will be under a Muslim Imam</u>, leader, <u>showing His complete adherence to Islam and assisting Allah in making all of humanity convert to Islam.</u>**

Islam believes in the return of Jesus the Messiah to earth, although his role and reason for His return is completely contrary to all that is taught in the Bible and believed by Christians. <u>Islam believes that His return is first and foremost to prove His mortality, and refute the false belief Christians hold about Him, as being God.</u> And He will live a normal life, marry, and also die as any other humans.

The differences between Islam's and the Christian's views of Jesus are vast and fundamental. <u>Muslims take great pains to assure the public of their beliefs that He was virgin born and that He preached the truth</u>. If we ask the average Muslim about his or her view of the historical Jesus they will tell you that everyone should honor the life of the great prophet. Yet, **every Muslim rejects Jesus Christ as God, Savior and the Coming Judge of the Universe.**

"AND BECAUSE OF THEIR SAYING (IN BOAST), "WE KILLED MESSIAH 'IESA (JESUS), SON OF MARYAM (MARY), THE MESSENGER OF ALLÂH," - BUT THEY KILLED HIM NOT, NOR CRUCIFIED HIM, BUT THE RESEMBLANCE OF 'IESA (JESUS) WAS PUT OVER ANOTHER MAN (AND THEY KILLED THAT MAN), AND THOSE WHO DIFFER THEREIN ARE FULL OF DOUBTS.

SURAH 4:157

8

Islam and **THE CRUCFIXION**

Christians have preached, taught and believed the crucifixion, death, burial and resurrection of Jesus for over two thousand years. Without the resurrection of Jesus Christ, we have no hope of salvation. Islam rejects these doctrines and offers a different account of what happened at the cross and afterwards. Islam believes that Jesus was merely one of Allah's many prophets or messengers, not "**God's only son**." Their version of the crucifixion portrays Allah as a horrible deceiver and **Jesus as the greatest failure** in the history of all the prophets. Muslims claim that "Allah is Truth" and that Jesus is to be revered as one of Allah's mightiest prophets. These claims are hollow and empty, for Islamic doctrine comes with unlimited heresy, simply because the Koran is a demonic book, filled with demonic deceptions, lies and allegorical un-truth, and half-truths. Doom awaits all who believe in its ideologies and teachings.

The Koran and The Crucifixion

Surah 4:155-156 "Because of their breaking the covenant, and of their rejecting the (proofs, evidences, verses, lessons, signs, revelations, etc.) of Allah, and of their killing the Prophets unjustly, and of their saying: 'Our hearts are wrapped.' (with coverings, i.e. we do not understand what the messengers say). Nay, Allah has set a seal upon their hearts because of their disbelief, so they believe not but a little. And because of their (Jews) disbelief and uttering against Mary a grave false charge (that she has committed illegal sexual intercourse;"

Surah 4:157-159 "And because of their saying (in boast), "We killed Messiah 'Iesa (Jesus), son of Maryam (Mary), the Messenger of Allâh," - but they killed him not, nor crucified him, but the resemblance of 'Iesa (Jesus) was put over another man (and they killed that man), and those who differ therein are full of doubts. They have no (certain) knowledge, they follow nothing but conjecture. For surely; they killed him not [i.e. 'Iesa (Jesus), son of Maryam (Mary)]: But Allâh raised him ['Iesa (Jesus)] up (with his body and soul) unto Himself (and he is in the heavens). And Allâh is Ever All-Powerful, AllWise. And there is none of the people of the Scripture (Jews and Christians), but must believe in him ['Iesa (Jesus), son of Maryam (Mary), as only a Messenger of Allâh and a human being], before his ['Iesa (Jesus) or a Jew's or a Christian's] death (at the time of the appearance of the angel of death). And on the Day of Resurrection, he ['Iesa (Jesus)] will be a witness against them."

These Koranic texts tell us that Jesus was lifted up to heaven after his enemies, the Jews, complained and misled the king, because they wanted to kill Him by crucifixion. Here we find a full demonic fabrication; Ibn Abu Hatim has narrated from Ibn Abbas saying:

> "When Allah wanted to lift him up to heaven, Jesus came to his companions in the house. There were twelve people, with some from among his disciples. He just had a bath, and his head was still dribbling with water." He said to them: 'There are those among you who will disbelieve in me twelve times after he had believed in me!' Then he said: 'Who will from among you take my likeness and be killed in my place, so will become in my rank?' A young youth came forwards. But Jesus said to him: 'Sit down! Then he repeated the same question, and the same youth stood up and came forward, and said: 'I.' Jesus said: 'You are the one,' and then the likeness of Jesus was put on him, and Jesus was lifted up to the heaven from the window of his house. Jews came looking for him. They took the youth and killed him and then crucified him."

The Koran teaches that Jesus is a wonderful, humble, generous messenger of Allah who came down and revealed Allah's words to his people, the people of Israel. **Muslims do not believe that Jesus is God**, nor do they believe that

God ever chose to come down to earth in the form of a man to die and become the payment for our sins and to forgive us. They reject Jesus as God come in the flesh as savior.

The universal **belief in Islam is that, Jesus never died on the cross**, never wanted to die on the cross, nor ever was born to die on the cross. This is a complete contradiction of what we find in the Bible. Muslims believe that Jesus was sentenced to death, and people just thought that he was crucified on the cross. The Koran rejects the crucifixion, and claims that it is false and a fabrication by Christians. According to Islam, Jesus never died on the cross, nor did he ever die for anyone's sins. What does the Koran actually say about the crucifixion of Jesus?

Surah 3:55 "And (remember) when Allah said: O Jesus! I will take you, and raise you to myself and clear you [of the forged statement that Jesus is Allah's son] of those who disbelieve; and I will make those who follow you (Monotheists, who worship none but Allah) superior to those who disbelieve [in the oneness of Allah, or disbelieve in some of his messengers, e.g. Muhammad, Jesus, Moses, etc. or in his Holy Books, e.g. The Torah, the Gospel, the Koran] til the Day of Resurrection. Then you will return to me, and I will judge between you in the matters in which you used to dispute."

According to the Koran, Allah promised to raise him to heaven. Jesus was charged by the Jews with blasphemy as claiming to be God or the son of God. The Christians have just adopted the substance of the fabricated claim of Jesus' crucifixion, and made it the cornerstone of the Christian faith. Islam believes that all of the controversies about dogma and faith will disappear when we appear before Allah. He will judge based on the belief and submission to Islam, **not Jesus!** The death, burial and resurrection of Jesus is totally rejected in Islam.

Surah 29:27 "And we bestowed upon him (Abraham, Issac and Jacob) and we ordained among his offspring the Prophethood and the Book [i.e. The Torah to Moses, the Gospel to Jesus and the Koran to Muhammad, all from the offspring of Abraham] and we granted him his reward in this world; and verily in the hereafter he is indeed among the righteous."

Surah 37:114-121 "And indeed we gave our grace to (Moses and Aaron). And we saved them and their people from great distress, and helped them so they became the victors. And we gave them the clear Scripture; and guided them to the right path. And we left for them (a goodly remembrance) among the later generations. Peace be upon Moses and Aaron! Verily thus do we reward the good-doers."

Surah 4:41-42 "How (will it be) when we bring from each nation a witness, and we bring you (O Muhammad) as a witness against these people? On that day those who disbelieved and disobeyed the Messenger (Muhammad) will wish that they were buried in the earth but they will never be able to hide a single fact from Allah."

In this Surah, Allah will judge people based on what their messengers had told them. Allah sent to nations and tribes, prophets and messengers to direct those people from the darkness of Satan, to the light of Allah. It's easy to see an attempt to parallel the text of Scripture, thus cause it to be believable and acceptable. Only a demonic book could attempt this level of deceit.

Surah 3:59 "Verily, the likeness of (Jesus) before **Allah is the likeness of Adam. He created him from dust**, then said to him: 'Be.' And he was."

Surah 4:171-172 "O People of the Scripture (Christians)! Do not exceed the limits in your religion: nor say of Allah aught but the truth. The Messiah (Jesus) the son of (Mary) was (no more than) a Messenger of Allah, And His Word, (Be-and he was) which He bestowed on Mary, and a Spirit created by Him: so believe In Allah and His Messengers. Say not "Three, (Trinity)" Cease! (It is) better for you. For Allah is (the only) One god, glory be to Him: (Far Exalted is He) above having a son. To Him (Allah) belongs all that is in the heavens and all that is in the earth. And Allah is All-sufficient as a Disposer of affairs."

Jesus and the Koran

The Koran states that Jesus was the son of a woman, Mary, and therefore a man, a messenger; a man with a mission from Allah, and therefore entitled to honor. A word bestowed on Mary, for he was created by Allah's word "Be" (kun in Arabic), and he was. <u>Jesus was just a spirit proceeding from Allah, but not Allah himself.</u> His life and his mission were more limited than in the case of some other Messengers. Though the Koran teaches that Jesus was a prophet, Islam also teaches that Muhammad was the last prophet and messenger of Allah. Thus as the final prophet, the foremost, his mission was for all of the world for all times (**Surah 4:35**). **Muslims must look to Muhammad and his life, not to Jesus for revelation and spiritual guidance.** Islam is demonic and deceptive, and anyone deceived thereby is doomed for eternity in Hell.

Also, the doctrine of the Trinity, equality with Allah, and son-ship, are repudiated as blasphemies.

Koran Contradiction on Jesus' Crucifixion

Surah 19:33 "And peace be upon me [Jesus] the day I was born, and the day that I die, and the day that I shall be raised alive!"

Christians believe that Jesus was God Himself, who came to earth, He was crucified on the cross to pay our sin debt, then resurrected from death back to life and ascended to heaven, and one day, He will return visually in victory and glory to this earth where He will rule for a thousand years.

The Koran completely rejects the doctrine of Jesus' crucifixion!

Muslims believe that Jesus was born from Mary, the Virgin, preached the word of Allah to the people of Israel, raised to Allah alive (even though he might have been put on the cross, but never actually died), will come back to earth again to fight the army of Satan and assist Allah in bringing all people to the Muslim religion. Therefore, should someone ask a Muslim if he believes Jesus is virgin born, ascended to Heaven and will one day return, the answer would be an emphatic "yes," but since they reject the incarnation, that Jesus is God, then yes is "not" sufficient. Again, a Muslim may sound Biblical, but it is another Jesus, another Gospel and another god.

Some Muslim scholars say that Jesus was not crucified. In **(Surah 4:157)**, it means that he was put on the cross but did not die, and others say that it means that he was not put on the cross itself and never died. Either way, it doesn't really matter whether he was put on the cross or not. The more important issue is that **in Islam, Jesus was not crucified**; did not die for the sins of all of humanity. Therefore, in Islamic ideology, Jesus Christ is not Savior or Redeemer of mankind.

The Teaching of The Koran On Jesus' Crucifixion

The Koran denies the crucifixion of Jesus and argues that it was a <u>Jesus look-alike that was crucified</u>.

Surah 4:157 "And because of their saying (in boast), we killed Messiah, Isa (Jesus) son of Maryam (Mary), the Messenger of Allah. But they killed him not, nor crucified him, but it appeared so to them [the resemblance of Isa (Jesus) was put over another man (and they killed that man)], and those who differ therein are full of doubts. They have no (certain) knowledge, they follow nothing but conjecture. For surely, they killed him not."

Muhammad Taught No Resurrection

Bukhari 4:657: Narrated Abu Huraira: Allah's Apostle said, "By Him in Whose Hands my soul is, surely (Jesus,) the son of Mary will soon descend amongst you and will judge mankind justly (as a Just Ruler); he will break the Cross and kill the pigs and there will be no Jizyah (i.e. taxation taken from non Muslims). Money will be in abundance so that nobody will accept it, and a single prostration to Allah (in prayer) will be better than the whole world and whatever is in it." Abu Huraira added "If you wish, you can recite (this verse of the Holy Book): -- 'And there is none Of the people of the Scriptures (Jews and Christians) But must believe in him (i.e. Jesus as an Apostle of Allah and a human being) Before his death. And on the Day of Judgment He will be a witness against them."

The Koran Teaches No Mediator

Surah 6:163-164 "He (Allah) has no partner. And of this I (Muhammad) have been commanded, and I am the first of the Muslims. Say: "shall I seek a lord other than Allah while he is lord of all things? No person earns any (sin) except against himself (only) and no bearer of burdens shall bear the burden of another. Then unto your lord is your return, so he will tell you that wherein you have been differing."

A Muslim Judged on Works

Surah 23:102-104 "Then, those whose scales (of good deeds) are heavy, they are the successful. And those whose scales (of good deeds) are light, they are those who lose their ownselves, in Hell will they abide. The Fire will burn their faces, and therein they will grin, with displaced (disfigured) lips."

The Contradiction of Muhammad

Muhammad contradicted himself in the Hadith when he said that he could serve as a mediator for some in Hell Fire and take them to Paradise.

Bukhari 9:532[c] Narrated Anas: The Prophet said, "The believers will be kept (waiting) on the Day of Resurrection so long that they will become worried and say, "Let us ask somebody to intercede for us with our Lord so that He may relieve us from our place...So they will come to me, (Muhammad) and I will ask my Lord's permission to enter His House and then I will be permitted. When I see Him I will fall down in prostration before Him, and He will leave me (in prostration) as long as He will, and then He will say, 'O Muhammad, lift up your head and speak, for you will be listened to, and intercede, for your intercession will be accepted, and ask (for anything) for it will be granted.' Then I will raise my head and glorify my Lord with certain praises which He has taught me. Allah will put a limit for me (to intercede for a certain type of people) I will take them out and make them enter Paradise." (Qatada said: I heard Anas saying that), the Prophet said, "I will go out and take them out of Hell (Fire) and let them enter Paradise, and then I will return and ask my Lord for permission to enter His House and I will be permitted..."

The Bible and Jesus' Crucifixion

John 19:14-20 "And it was the preparation of the Passover, and about the sixth hour: and he saith unto the Jews, Behold your King! But they cried out, Away with him, away with him, crucify him. Pilate saith unto them, Shall I crucify your King? The chief priests answered, we have no king but Caesar. Then delivered he him therefore unto them to be crucified. And they took Jesus, and led him away. And he bearing his cross went forth into a place called the place of a skull, which is called in the Hebrew Golgotha, where they crucified him, and two others with him, on either side one, and Jesus in the midst. And Pilate wrote a title, and put it on the cross. And the writing was, JESUS OF NAZARETH THE KING OF THE JEWS. This title then read many of the Jews: for the place where Jesus was crucified was nigh to the city: and it was written in Hebrew, and Greek, and Latin."

Paul Taught that Jesus was crucified

1 Corinthians 2:2 "For I determined not to know any thing among you, save Jesus Christ, and him crucified."

The Bible Teaches that Jesus was God's Sin Offering

Hebrews 9:28 "So Christ was once offered to bear the sins of many; and unto them that look for him shall he appear the second time without sin unto salvation."

1 Peter 2:24 "Who his own self bare our sins in his own body on the tree, that we, being dead to sins, should live unto righteousness: by whose stripes ye were healed."

Jesus' Crucifixion: "Fact Or Fiction?"

Another of the conflicts between Christians and Muslims is the authenticity of the crucifixion of Christ. Since the crucifixion is a main doctrine of the church, it is imperative that every Christian knows what God's Word, the Bible says. Read it, believe, preach it, practice it, and proclaim it to the whole world. Jesus Himself said He would be crucified (**Matt. 20:17-20**).

The Old Testament Prophecies; Jesus' Crucifixion

There are over forty-seven prophecies in the Old Testament concerning the death of Christ on the cross, all of which were literally fulfilled. We also have the testimony of all of the New Testament writers, and the testimony of Jesus Himself of His crucifixion. Are we to believe the lie of the Koran, Muhammad, the moon god Allah, rather than God's word, the Bible? Islam is a demonic lie that must be rejected. May God help us as a nation to recognize Islam as a national threat to our security.

"WHEN SHE BRINGS THE BABY
TO HER PEOPLE, THEY SAID
MARY TRULY A STRANGE THING
HAS THOU BROUGHT O SISTER
OF AARON THY FATHER WAS
NOT A MAN OF EVIL NOR THY
MOTHER A WOMAN UNCHASTE."

SURAH 19:27-28

9

Islam and MARY

Most Muslims will remind you continually that the Koran teaches about Maryam (Mary), the mother of Jesus. The Koran uses the names Maryam (Mary) more than 34 times. From all of these people, one of them is Mary, the mother of Jesus, and the other is the wife of Pharaoh. Aisha and Mary have reached the level of perfection as no other woman, according to the Hadith.

Bukhari 4:643 narrated by Abu-musa Al-Ashari the prophet said "The superiority of Aisha to other ladies is like the superiority of Tharid, (i.e. the meat and bread dish) to other meals. Many men reached the level of perfection but no other woman reached such a level except Maryam (Mary), the daughter of Imran, and Asiya-the wife of Pharaoh. Maryam (Mary) and Pharaoh's wife, Asiya, are examples."

Surah 66:11-12 "And Allah has set forth an example for those who believe: the wife of Fir'aun (Pharaoh) when she said, My Lord build for me a home with you in paradise and save me from, Fir'aum (Pharaoh) and his work and save me from the people who are (polytheists, wrongdoers and disbelievers in Allah). And Maryam (Mary) the daughter of Imran who guarded her chastity. And we breathed into (the sleeve of her shirt or her garment) through (Gabriel) and she testified to the truth of the words of her Lord, (believed in the words of Allah) 'be'-and he was, that is, son of Maryam (Mary) as <u>a messenger of Allah</u> and also believed in his scriptures, and she was obedient to Allah."

Mary According to the Koran

Surah 3:35 "(Remember) when the wife of Imran said, o my Lord I have vowed to you what (the child that) is in my womb to be dedicated for your services (free from all worldly work to serve your place of worship) so accept this from me. Verily, you are the all-hearer, the all knowing".

Surah 3:36 "Then when she gave birth to her child (Mary) she said, **'o my Lord I am delivered of a female child.'** And Allah knew better what she brought forth, and the male is not like the female, and I have named her Maryam (Mary), and I seek refuge with Allah for her and for her offspring from (Satan) the outcast."

Surah3:37 "...So her lord (Allah) accepted her with a goodly acceptance. He made her grow in a good manner and put her under the care of Zechariah. Every time he entered her room, to visit her, he found her supplied with sustenance. He said O Maryam (Mary)! From where have you got this? She said this is from Allah. Verily Allah provides sustenance to whom he wills without limit.

The Koran discusses Mary's miraculous conception as well the story of Mary when she withdrew from her family to a place in the west side of the town.

Surah 19:16-17 "And mention in the Book (Koran O Muhammad the story of Maryam (Mary), when she withdrew in seclusion from her family to a place facing east. She placed a screen (to screen herself) from them; then we sent her Gabriel, and he appeared before her in the form of a man in all respects."

Surah 19:19 "(The angel) said I am only a messenger from your lord, (to announce) to you the gift of a righteous son."

Surah 19:20 "She said: How can I have a son, when no man has touched me, nor am I unchaste?"

Surah 19:21 "He said So (it will be) your lord said that is easy for me...."

Surah 19:22 "So she conceived him, and she withdrew with him to a far place (i.e. Bethlehem valley about 4-6 miles away from Jerusalem)."

Surah 19:23 "and the pains of child birth drove her to the trunk of a date-palm she said; would that I had died before this and had been forgotten and out of sight."

Surah 19:24-26 "but a voice cried to her from beneath of the palm-tree grieve not for your Lord has provided a water stream under you. And shake the trunk of the date-palm towards you, it will let fall fresh ripe dates upon you. So eat and drink and be glad. And if you see any human being say Verily, I have vowed a fast unto the most gracious (Allah) so I shall not speak to any human beings this day."

Mary, Sister of Aaron

Joseph is not mentioned in the Koran but <u>the Mary of the Koran mentioned to us is the sister of Aaron</u>.

Surah 19:27-28 "When she brings the baby to her people, they said Maryam (Mary) truly a strange thing has thou brought o sister of Aaron thy father was not a man of evil nor thy mother a woman unchaste."

Surah 19:29 "Then she pointed to him. They said how can we talk to one who is a child in the cradle?"

Surah 19:30-33 "He (Jesus) said "Verily, I am a slave of Allah, he has given me the Scripture and me a prophet, and he has made me

108

blessed wheresoever I be, and had enjoined on me prayer and charity as long as I live. And dutiful to my mother and made me not arrogant, unblest. And peace be upon me the day I was born, the day that I die, and the day that I shall be raised alive!"

Surah 21:91 "And she who guarded her chastity [Virgin Mary]: We breathed into (the sleeves of) her (shirt or garment) through (Gabriel) and we made her and her son (Jesus) a sign for (the mankind and jinn)."

Surah 66:12 "And Maryam (Mary), the daughter of Imran who guarded her chasitity. And we breathed into the sleeve of her shirt or her garment through Gabriel and she testified to the truth of the words of her Lord [i.e. believed in the words of Allah, be- and he was-that is (Jesus), son of Mary as a messenger of Allah] and (also believed in) his Scriptures, and she was of the obedient to Allah."

Although Mary is viewed in honor, she is not God, nor to be worshiped; is not the Virgin Mary of Holy Scripture? According to the Holy Bible, Mary was simply a chosen vessel through which God sent His son, thus providing His humanity, to identify with man, thereby providing a way for man to be saved by faith through Christ's finished work on the cross. Mary is not to be deified as in some religious denominations, but recognized as God's chosen vessel.

Most Christians when hearing the Islamic praise for Mary will be deluded into believing that Islam may be Biblical. *Never, never* accept any Islamic teaching as Godly! One other thing: Mary is "not" the mother of God as some Christian cults teach today!!

10

Islam and SALVATION

Islam teaches that only those who are true believers in Allah and his prophet Muhammad will go to heaven. Salvation in Islam is therefore achieved by submission to the teachings of the Koran. **All non-Muslims, according to Islam are losers and cursed of Allah, thus are destined to go to Hell.** According to the Koran, there are **four basic points** to illustrate what Islam believes about salvation. Salvation is:

1. Based on acceptance of Allah and Muhammad, everyone else will go to Hell. Acceptance of a false god.

2. Based on good works, "every soul shall be paid in full what he has earned (works salvation).

3. Based on personal merit, "Allah loves those who cleanse themselves," (must be good enough).

4. Predestined by Allah, Muslims have no assurance of Heaven. Allah may or may not predestine them to go to Heaven.

Surah 4:49 "Have you not seen those Jews and Christians who claim sanctity for themselves. Nay but Allah sanctifies whom he wills and they will not be dealt with injustice even equal to the extent of scalish thread in the long slit of a date stone."

Surah 24:21 "O you who believe! Follow not the footsteps of Satan. And whosoever follows the footsteps of Satan then verily he commands (to commit sexual indecency and [disbelief and polytheism (i.e. to do evil and wicked deeds; and to speak or do what is forbidden in Islam)] And had it not been for the grace of Allah and his mercy on you, not one of you would ever be pure from sins. But Allah purifies (guides to Islam) whom he wills, and Allah is the all-hearer, all-knower."

Surah 57:22 "No calamity befalls on the earth or in yourselves but it is inscribed in the book of decrees before we bring it into existence. Verily that is easy for Allah."

The Koran teaches the necessity of both faith in Allah and good work for salvation and by obeying to the prophet Muhammad, by carrying out the five pillars of Islam.

Surah 33:43 "He it is who sends (his blessings) on you and his angels too (ask Allah to bless and forgive you) that he may bring you out from darkness (of disbelief and polytheism) into light (of belief and Islamic monotheism) and he is ever merciful to the believers."

Surah 41:30 "Verily those who say our lord is Allah (alone) and then they stand firm, on them the angels will descend (at the time of their death) saying fear not nor grieve! But receive the glad tidings of Paradise which you have been promised."

Surah 3:131 "And fear the fire, which is prepared for the disbelievers (non-Muslims)."

Surah 2:177 'It is not (piety, righteousness and every act of obedience to Allah, etc.) that you turn your faces towards east and or west (in prayers) but righteousness is (the quality of) the one who believes in Allah and the Last Day, the Angels, the book and the Prophets and gives his wealth in spite of love for it to his kinsfolk, to the orphans, or for the wayfarer, for those who ask, and to set slaves free, performs prayer and gives charity, and fulfill their covenants when they make it, and those who are patient in extreme poverty and ailment (disease) and at the time of fighting (during the battles). Such are the people of the truth and they are the pious."

Surah 57:21 "Race with another in hastening towards forgiveness from your lord (Allah), and paradise the width whereof is as the width of Heaven and the earth, prepared for those who believe in Allah and his messengers. That is the grace of Allah which he bestows on whom he is pleased with. And Allah is the owner of great bounty."

Surah 4:13-14 "These are limits (set by) Allah (or ordainments as regards laws of inheritance) and whosoever obeys Allah and his messenger (Muhammad) will be admitted to the gardens under which rivers flow (in Paradise) to abide therein and that will be great success. And whosoever disobeys Allah and his messenger and transgress his limits he will cast him into the fire to abide therein and he shall have a disgraceful torment."

No Assurance of Salvation

In many places in the Koran, Muslims are promised that if they do what is right and fear Allah, then they will be granted entrance into paradise. If they don't, then hell will be their abode.

Surah 2:25 "And give glad tidings *to those who believe and do righteous good deeds*; that for them will be Gardens under which rivers flow (Paradise). Every time they will be provided fruit therefrom, they will say: this is what we were provided with before; and they will be given things in resemblance (i.e. the same form but in different taste). And they shall have therein (purified mates or wives); and abide therein forever."

Surah 2:81-82 "Yes, whosoever earns evil, and his sin has surrounded him, they are dwellers of the Fire. They will dwell therein forever. And those who believe (in the oneness of Allah-Islamic monotheism) and do righteous good deeds, they are dwellers of Paradise, they will dwell therein forever."

Surah 33:35 "...Men and women who have surrendered, believing men and believing women, *obedient men and obedient women*, truthful men and truthful women, enduring men and enduring women, humble men and humble women, men and women *who give in charity*, men who fast and women *who fast*, men and women who guard their private parts, men and women who remember Allah oft-for them Allah has prepared forgiveness and a great reward (Paradise)."

This clearly presupposes that salvation according to Islam is the result of having true faith and doing good works according to the Koran; that is salvation is obtained by believing and doing all that the Koran says. Keep in mind the Koran advocates jihad, (killing non-Muslims) to be assured salvation.

Allah Predestines

But other texts and the so-called scholars of Islam teach something quite different; in fact they present a rather incoherent and contradictory view of the means of salvation. For example, the Koran claims that it is purely the grace of Allah that purifies a person:

Surah 24:21 "O you who believe! Follow not the footsteps of Satan. And whosoever follows the footsteps of Satan then verily he commands (to commit sexual indecency and [disbelief and polytheism (i.e. to do evil and wicked deeds; and to speak or do what is forbidden in Islam)] And had it not been for the grace of Allah and his mercy on you, not one of you would ever be pure from sins. But Allah purifies (guides to Islam) whom he wills, and Allah is the all-hearer, all-knower."

This, perhaps, explains why Muhammad supposedly taught that good works couldn't save a person:

Bukhari 7:577 Narrated Abu Huraira: "I heard Allah's Apostle saying, *'The good deeds of any person will not make him enter Paradise.' (i.e., none can enter Paradise through his good deeds.)* They (the Prophet's companions) said, "Not even you, O Allah's Apostle?" He said, *"Not even myself, unless Allah bestows His favor and mercy on me."* So be moderate in your religious deeds and do the deeds that are within your ability: and none of you should wish for death, for if he is a good doer, he may increase his good deeds, and if he is an evil doer, he may repent to Allah."

Bukhari 8:474 Narrated Aisha, "The Prophet said, 'Do good deeds properly, sincerely and moderately, and receive good news *because one's good deeds will NOT make him enter*

Paradise." They asked, "Even you, O Allah's Apostle?" He said, "*Even I, unless and until Allah bestows His pardon and Mercy on me.*"

Moreover, certain reports claim that a Muslim who dies confessing the Shahadah, the Islamic profession of faith that there is no god except Allah, will enter paradise even if he or she has lived a grossly immoral life!

Bukhari 7:717 Narrated Abu Dharr: "I came to the Prophet while he was wearing white clothes and sleeping. Then I went back to him again after he had got up from his sleep. He said, "Nobody says: 'None has the right to be worshipped but Allah' and then later on he dies while believing in that, except that he will enter Paradise." **I said, "Even if he had committed illegal sexual intercourse and theft?"** I said, "Even If he had committed illegal sexual intercourse and theft." He said, "Even If he had committed Illegal sexual intercourse and theft, in spite of the Abu Dharr's dislikeness."** Abu 'Abdullah said, "This is at the time of death or before it; if one repents and regrets and says 'None has the right to be worshipped but Allah', he will be forgiven his sins."

Bukhari 9:579 Narrated Abu Dharr: "The Prophet said, Gabriel came to me and gave me the glad tidings that anyone who died without worshipping anything besides Allah, would enter Paradise. I asked (Gabriel), 'Even if he committed theft, and even if he committed illegal sexual intercourse?' **He said, (Yes), even if he committed theft, and even if he committed illegal sexual intercourse.**"

Contradictions About Salvation

The above assertion that a person's repentance at death will be accepted contradicts the express teachings of the Koran:

Surah 4:17-18 "Allah accepts only the repentance *of those who do evil in ignorance,* **and foolishness** *then repent soon afterwards*, it is they whom Allah will forgive, and Allah is ever Knowing, Wise. And of no effect is the repentance for those *who go on doing evil deeds, until death faces one of them*, and he says: now, I repent; nor those who die while they are disbelievers. For them We have prepared a painful torment."

Surah 40:84-85 "So when they saw Our punishment, they said: "We believe in Allah alone and reject (all) that we used to associate with Him as (His) partners. Then *their Faith (in Islamic Monotheism) could not avail them when they saw Our punishment. (Like) this has been the way of Allah in dealing with His slaves.* And there the disbelievers lost utterly (when our torment covered them)."

According to the above, Allah does not and will not accept the repentance of a person at death unlike the God

of the Bible. <u>Remember the thief on the cross next to Jesus at His crucifixion, called on Jesus by faith, and Jesus assured him of Heaven</u> (Lk. 23:39-43).

There are other narrations claiming that Allah will cast Jews and Christians into hell in the place of the Muslims!

Christians Go To Hell For Muslims

Muslim 037:6665 "Abu Musa' reported that Allah's Messenger (may peace be upon him) said: When it will be the Day of Resurrection Allah would deliver to every Muslim **a Jew or a Christian and say: That is your *RESCUE* from Hell-Fire**."

Muslim 037:6666 "Abu Burda reported on the authority of his father that Allah's Apostle (may peace be upon him) said: **No Muslim would die but Allah would admit *IN HIS STEAD* a Jew or a Christian in Hell-Fire**. 'Umar b. Abd al-'Aziz took an oath: By One besides Whom there is no god but He, <u>thrice that his father had narrated that to him from Allah's Messenger</u> (may peace be upon him)."

Muslim 037:6668 "Abu Burda reported Allah's Messenger (may peace be upon him) as saying: **There would come people amongst the Muslims on the Day of Resurrection with *AS HEAVY SINS AS A MOUNTAIN*, and Allah would *FORGIVE THEM* and He would *PLACE IN THEIR STEAD* the Jews and the Christians**. (As far as I think), Abu Raub said: I do not know as to

119

who is in doubt. Abu Burda said: I narrated it to 'Umar b. 'Abd al-'Aziz, whereupon he said: Was it your father who narrated it to you from Allah's Apostle (may peace be upon him)?"

No Real Atonement

Allah is going to ransom Muslims from their sins by <u>**punishing the Jews and Christians in their stead,**</u> **which is nothing more than a form of vicarious atonement! Moreover, why are Muslims saved by faith in the Islamic creed alone in spite of being grossly immoral and wicked?** <u>**The Jews and Christians will be punished for the sins of these Muslims!**</u>

Muhammad is Savior

The hadiths further teach that Muslims are saved not on the basis of their good works, or because a Jew or Christian will be punished in their place, but because of Muhammad's intercession: <u>**Thus, Muhammad is Savior!**</u>

Bukhari 2:553 " Narrated 'Abdullah bin 'Umar: The Prophet said, "A man keeps on asking others for something till he comes on the Day of Resurrection without any piece of flesh on his face." The Prophet added, "On the Day of Resurrection, the Sun will come near (to the people) to such an extent that the sweat will reach up to the middle of the ears, so, when all the people are in that state, they will ask Adam for help, and then Moses, and then Muhammad (p.b.u.h)." The sub-narrator added "**Muhammad will intercede with Allah to judge amongst the people**. He will proceed on till he will hold the ring of the door (of Paradise) **and then Allah will exalt him to Maqam Muhammad (the privilege of intercession, etc.)**. And all the people of the gathering will send their praises to Allah".

Muhammad is Intercessor

Muhammad even stated that his intercession would be for those Muslims who commit major sins, i.e. adultery, murder etc.

Dawud 40:4721 Narrated Anas ibn Malik: "The Prophet said: My intercession will be for those of my people who have committed major sins."

What this essentially means is that Allah will forgive rapists, adulterers, murders etc. all because of Muhammad's intercession, indicating that it really doesn't matter how a Muslim lives, whether he or she decides to live a righteous life or a very wicked and immoral one. Simply put, Muhammad is seen as a divine savior, thus displacing Jesus Christ and enthroning himself. Jesus Christ is our only mediator between God and man.

All that matters is that he or she dies professing faith in Islamic monotheism since this is all that is needed for Allah to grant such a person entrance into paradise.

Koranic Contradictions About Salvation

Yet Muhammad's intercession introduces another contradiction with the Koran since it expressly denies that there is any intercessor besides Allah. Islam rejects Jesus as savior, and they deny the resurrection, therefore there is no probability of salvation. *The Koran contradicts itself because it is a demonic, satanic lie.*

Surah 6:51 "And warn therewith (the Koran) those who fear they shall be gathered before their Lord; where there will be neither A *protector nor an intercessor for them besides Him*; so they may fear Allah."

Surah 6:70 "And leave alone those who take their religion as play and amusement, and whom the life of this world has deceived. But, (remind) them with it (the Koran), lest a person be given up to destruction for that which he has earned; when he will find for himself *NO protector and no intercessor besides Allah,*; and even if he offers every ransom, it will not be accepted from him. Such are they who are given up to destruction because of that which they have earned. For them will be a drink of boiling water and a painful torment because they used to disbelieve."

Surah 32:4 "Allah is He who created the heavens and the earth, and all that is between them in six days. Then He rose over the Throne (in a manner that suits his majesty). You (mankind) have none besides *Him, as a* *protector or helper or an intercessor.* Will you not then remember (or receive admonition?"

Muhammad Not Sure of Salvation

The Koran even contradicts other Surahs and narrations where Muhammad himself didn't know whether he was saved, let alone whether he could save anyone else!

Surah 46:9 "Say (O Muhammad) I am not a new thing among the Messengers (of Allah) (i.e. I am not the first Messenger) *nor do I know what will be done with me or with you.* I only follow that which is revealed to me, and I am but a plain warner."

Bukhari 4:16 Narrated Abu Huraira: "When Allah revealed the Verse: 'Warn your nearest kinsmen,' Allah's Apostle got up and said, "O people of Quraish (or said similar words)! Buy (i.e. save) yourselves (from the Hellfire) **as I cannot save you from Allah's Punishment**; O Bani Abd Manaf! **I cannot save you from Allah's Punishment**, O Safiya, the Aunt of Allah's Apostle! I cannot save you from Allah's Punishment; **O Fatima bint Muhammad! Ask me anything from my wealth, but I cannot save you from Allah's Punishment**."

In Islam, there is no salvation because there is no Savior (Jesus). There is no assurance of salvation in Islam. A Muslim will spend his or her life in attempting to please

Allah with good works as giving to the poor, praying five times a day toward Mecca, and going on his once in a lifetime pilgrimage to Mecca, or committing Jihad. Yet, he can never be sure of Heaven. Even Muhammad was not sure he would go to Heaven. **The Koran teaches that Allah forgives only those he chooses and no Muslim can be sure that he is chosen.** Islam teaches that in the Day of Judgment, all works and deeds will be placed on the scales and weighed; good works are heavy and evil deeds are light. **There is only one sure way for a Muslim to go to Heaven, and that is by carrying out an act of jihad, thus dying for Allah, to be assured of Heaven.**

In Jihad or Holy War, defending Islam and attempting to destroy all non-Muslims, one can be assured of salvation. **"If you are slain or die in Allah's way...it is unto Allah, you shall be taken."** Satan is the master deceiver.

11

Islam and HELL

The Koran teaches that there is a hell. It is a place of torment; however, it will cease to exist according to Islamic teaching when the last repentant Muslim sinner leaves it to enter paradise.

According to the Koran the tortures of the fire are fearful, it has crackling and roaring flames, fierce boiling waters, scorching wind, and black smoke. Very much like Dante's "Inferno," the inhabitants sigh and wail; anguished in their torment, their scorched skins exchanged for new ones so that they can encounter the pain again and again. They try to escape, but cannot.Notice some of the equally vivid and materialistic descriptions of hell that are found throughout the Koran:

There are nearly 500 texts from 87 Surahs that speak of Hell. Here are just a few examples:

Surah 40:71-72 "When iron collars will be
rounded over their necks and the chains,

they shall be dragged along in the boiling water, then they will be burned in the fire."

Surah 22:19-21 "…then as for those who disbelieved, garments of fire shall be cut out for them, boiling water will be poured over their heads. With it will melt (or vanish away) what is within their bellies, as well as (their) skins. And for them are hooked rods of iron (to punish them)."

Surah 4:56 "Surely! Those who disbelieved in our revelations, we shall burn them in fire. As often as their skins are roasted through, we shall change them for other skins that they may taste the punishment. Truly Allah is ever Most Powerful, All-Wise."

Surah 56:92-94 "But if he (the dying person) be of the denying (of the Resurrection), the erring, (away from the right path of Islamic monotheism) then for him is an entertainment with boiling water. And burning in hell fire."

Surah 9:73 ""O Prophet (Muhammad)! Strive hard against the disbelievers (non-Muslims) and the hypocrites and be harsh against them; their abode is hell, and worst indeed is that destination."

Surah 66:9 "O Prophet (Muhammad)! Strive against the disbelievers (non-Muslims) and hypocrites, and be severe against them. Their abode will be Hell and worst indeed is that destination."

Surah 8:55 "Verily the worst moving (living) creatures before Allah are those who disbelieve, (non-Muslims) so they shall not believe."

Surah 9:30 "And the Jews say, 'Ezra is the son of Allah,' and the Christians say: 'The Messiah is the son of Allah.' That is their saying with their mouths, resembling the saying of those who disbelieved aforetime. Allah's curse be on them, how they are deluded away from the truth!"

Surah 4:52 "They are those (Christians) whom Allah has *cursed*.."

Surah 4:47 "O, you who have been given the Scripture (Jews and Christians)! Believe in what we have revealed, (to Muhammad) confirming what is (already) with you, before we efface faces (by making them like the back of necks; without nose, mouth, eyes), and turn them hindwards, or curse them as we cursed the Sabbath-breakers. And the commandment of Allah is always executed."

This Surah speaks of the belief of the Muslims that Jews are descendants of swine and apes, since it says that wicked Jews (at least) were transformed by Allah in the past.

There are hundreds of Surahs that speak of violence and hatred against non-Muslims, particularly <u>Allah's dislike, manifested by his plans to physically torture non-Muslims for eternity in hell</u>. On one occasion when this writer was confronted by an Islamic because of our campus marquee that stated, "Muhammad taught murder, Jesus taught peace." The Muslim man told me that Allah would send me to Hell.

Bukhari 54:487   Someone asked, "O Allah's apostle this (ordinary) fire would have been sufficient (to torture the unbelievers)." Allah's apostle said, "The hell fire has 69 parts more than the ordinary (worldly) fire, each part is as hot as this (worldly) fire."

In other words, ordinary hell fire is not hot enough to torture non-Muslims.   Therefore, hell is 69 times hotter.   This vivifies the extreme hatred Islam has for all non-Muslims.

Bukhari 2:28   "Women comprise the majority of Hell's occupants".   (A weak Hadith, Kanz al-'ummal, 22:10, even suggests that 99% of women go to Hell.)

Muslim 40:6831   Non-Muslims in Hell will be given thick skin so as to prolong their agony (before they are given fresh skin for a new round of torture).

Bukhari 5:727   ...Allah's apostle [said] "Allah's curse be on the Jews and the Christians..."

This was spoken on Muhammad's death bed, and was one of the last things he ever said.

The Koran also contains dozens of Surahs that specifically describe Jews in the ugliest, most hateful terms. **These parts of the Koran are indistinguishable from any hate literature.** Islamic teaching from the Koran constitutes "hate crimes" in the highest sense of the term, yet is allowed and protected by the politically correct crowd today. America is not properly represented in Washington. We are constantly told that Islam is "**a peaceful religion**." We must have leaders that will stand and warn our nation of the coming Islamic invasion and enact laws to protect America "**NOW**."

Someone said, Hell, according to the Koran, has 7 gates and is composed of 7 stories forming a vast crater. Above is a bridge, named Sirat, spanning the whole length across it. This bridge which is sharper than the edge of a sword and thinner than a hair has to be crossed by the souls in order to enter Paradise.

The souls of the righteous Muslims cross it in a moment; those of ordinary righteous people take a longer or shorter time to cross it, while those of the unrighteous (non-Muslims) do not reach paradise but fall into the gulf. Faithful Muslims believed that they will cross over it in the "twinkling of an eye" and enter Paradise. Other Muslims may fall into Hell, but will later be released. Unbelievers (all non-Muslims) will fall into Hell and remain there forever.

The Koran speaks at length of the evil deeds for which those who will abide in the Hell forever deserve their never-ending fate. The response will be that they deserved Hell because they disbelieved in the Messenger (Muhammad) and his Message, that is all non-Muslims.

Notice some of the most heinous sins and crimes according to Islam:

Those Who Reject Islam-In Hell

Surah 21:96-101 "Until when Gog and Magog are
let loose (from their barrier) and they swoop
down from every mound. And the true
promise (Day of Resurrection) shall draw
near (of fulfillment). Then (when mankind
is resurrected from their graves), you shall
see the eyes of the disbelievers fixedly
staring in horror. (They will say:) Woe to
us! We were indeed heedless of this, nay
but we were polytheists and wrongdoers.
Certainly you (disbelievers) and that which
you are, worshipping now besides Allah are
(but) fuel for Hell! Surely you will enter it.
Had these (idols) been gods they would not
have entered there (Hell), and all of them
would abide therein. Therein they will be
breathing out with deep sighs and roaring
and therein they will hear not. Verily, those
for whom the good has preceded from us,
they will be removed far therefrom
(Hell)..."

Allah does not accept any religion other than Islam.
"And whoever seeks a religion other than Islam, it will not be
accepted from him and he will be one of the losers in the
Hereafter," in Hell.

All Non-Muslims in Hell

Muslims believe that all of the non-Muslims will be sent to Hell. Those who die while not believing that "There is no true god but Allah, and Muhammad is the Messenger (Prophet) of Allah" or are not Muslim will lose Paradise forever and will be sent to Hellfire.

Then as to those who disbelieve, Allah will chastise them with severe chastisement in this world and the hereafter, and they shall have no helpers.

Because the disbelievers (all non-Muslims) and polytheists (all Christians as viewed by Islam) will remain in Hell forever, it is considered to be their abode or dwelling place, just as Paradise is the abode of all Muslims.

O Prophet! Strive hard against the unbelievers (non-Muslims) and the hypocrites, and be hard against them; and their abode is hell; and evil is the resort.

Their abode will be the Fire; and evil is the home of the wrongdoers.

Surely, we have prepared for the unbelievers (non-Muslims) chains and shackles and a burning fire.

Who are some of these people who disbelieve? "Surely those who disbelieve from among the followers of the Book (Jews) and the polytheists (Christians) shall be in the fire of hell, abiding therein; they are the worst of men."

Here, "followers of The Book" and "polytheists" refer to Jews and Christians. **Therefore, according to the prophet Muhammad, Christians, Jews, and pagans are the vilest of all creatures in the world and will spend eternity in hell.**

Again it is necessary to understand that every Muslim believes that all Christians and Jews are wicked, evil and deserving of Hell. Only the Muslims are deserving of Paradise (Heaven).

The Bible teaches that all who reject the Lord Jesus Christ will be cast into Hell for eternity regardless of ethnicity, race or religion.

ISLAM TOTALLY REJECTS THE CHRISTIAN DOCTRINE OF THE TRINITY.

12

Islam and **THE TRINITY**

The Trinity, however complex a subject which cannot be fully appreciated or understood with the natural human mind, but revealed through the pages of the Bible and accepted by the Christian through faith. We will not attempt to go into full theological detail here. The trinity of the Godhead is a real and vital Biblical, theological truth. God the Father, God the Son, God the Holy Spirit are all three, yet one God. This subject is fully developed in this writer's book, "**Could Jesus Sin**," *the doctrine of the impeccability of Christ*.

The most crucial point to stress to Muslims is that true Christianity is based on Trinitarian monotheism, NOT tri-theism. Secondly, it is important to explain that it is the Holy Spirit (not Mary) that is the third Member of the Trinity. It is important because the Koran indicates that Mary is made to be a god, and is accepted in the mind of the Muslim, which obviously is problematic, to say the least.

Therefore, it is imperative to point out that Mary is not given divine status in the Bible and has not ever been given divine status within true Biblical Christianity. Mary was simply God's chosen vessel through which Jesus received His humanity.

Christ's Dual Nature

Jesus Christ is 100% God and 100% human; the welding together of Jesus' two natures without any mixture or deterioration of either. It is therefore needful to delve into the topic of Christ's Incarnation to some degree. A good knowledge of this is needful to further dispel the Koranic deception. God did not have sexual relations with Mary to beget Jesus. Christians do not believe this nor have they ever believed this. This point cannot be stressed enough. We can see how this misunderstanding of Christianity led to the recording of the Surahs within the pages of the Koran.

What Christians DO believe is that Jesus, being God, has existed eternally and entered the human race through a miraculous, NON-sexual Virgin Mary's conception. The miracle of the Virgin Birth is the work of the Holy Spirit (**Luke 1:26-33**). This event is what Christians refer to as the Incarnation. The apostle John gives an informative account of this in the following passage: "In the beginning was the Word, and the Word was with God, and the Word was God. The same was in the beginning with God. All things were made by him; and without him was not any thing made that was made..." (**John 1:1-3**) "And the Word was made flesh, and dwelt among us, (and we beheld his glory, the glory as of the only begotten of the Father,) full of grace and truth" (**John 1:14**). The apostle Paul, author of Hebrews, describes the Christology of Jesus in the following way:

> **"GOD, who at sundry times and in diverse manners spoke in time past unto the fathers by the prophets, Hath in these last days spoken unto us by his Son, whom he hath appointed heir of all things, by whom also he made the worlds; Who being the brightness of his glory, and the express image of his person, and upholding all things by the word of his Power, when he had by himself purged our sins, sat down on the right hand of the Majesty on high;"(Hebrews 1:1-3)**

We find that the Bible describes Jesus as being equal with God and as being God. Christians believe that Jesus is eternal and, therefore, was not only living before Mary's virginal conception, but also living before the foundations of the heaven and Earth were established. It was Jesus that is Creator of all things, according to **Colossians 1:15-20**. While Jesus maintained His divine nature when He entered the womb of Mary and all throughout His life on Earth, He also took on a human nature. Here, we have another complex fact of a Man that was both 100% divine and 100% human. While much could be and has been written on this subject, it is not the goal of this chapter to delve too deeply into it here. However, it may be appropriate to briefly expound on the Biblical explanation of Christ's dual nature. Jesus' humanity

135

was provided through Mary, His mother. It was God, The Holy Spirit, who impregnated Mary; (without any sexual relationship); thus God is the Father (**Lk. 1:26-33**). Jesus had a divine nature while, at the same time, entering human flesh and making Himself subject to the same laws and absolutes that He Himself established. It was His purpose to impeccably fulfill the Commandments of God and serve as a perfect Sacrifice that would provide the way for us to be saved through His perfect righteousness, which is the only way to be made holy before a Holy God. A full examination can be found in this author's book, "**Could Jesus Sin?**" Jesus had no sin, did no sin, and could do no sin; He is high, holy, harmless and undefiled.

Some ask, if Jesus was indeed divine, why He prayed, Who He was praying to, and Who He was crying out to on the cross. Consider the following passages:

> "**And he went a little farther, and fell on his face,** *and prayed*, **saying,** *O my Father, if it be possible, let this cup pass from me: nevertheless not as I will, but as thou wilt.*"**(Matthew 26:39)"**

> "**And about the ninth hour Jesus cried with a loud voice, saying, Eli, Eli, lama sabachthani? That is to say,** *MyGod, my God, why hast thou forsaken me?*"**(Matthew 27:46)

We see in these passages clearly that Jesus was praying. With a reasonable understanding of the Trinity, it is obvious here that Jesus in His humanity is talking with His Father in

Heaven. In these particular texts, we can see His human anxiety as He faced the crucifixion. It was almost time for Jesus to consummate His mission by serving as the perfect, sinless Sacrifice for the sin of all in the world. The human anxiety that clearly burdened the Lord in this case is a manifestation of His human nature. However, being the ultimate picture of piety, obedience, and perseverance that He is, He completed the purpose of His mission, by dying on the cross and being resurrected on Sunday, thereby creating the bridge of reconciliation between man and God. Jesus' purpose for coming into this world was to die, shed His rich, red, royal blood on a cruel Roman cross for the redemption of humanity for "**whosoever will**."

Another question that is often posed is, "Why did Jesus consider the Father to be greater than Himself?" The following verse gives us a good depiction of this:

> **"Ye have heard how I said unto you, I go away, and come again unto you. If ye loved me, ye would rejoice, because I said, I go unto the Father: for my Father is greater than I." (John 14:28)**

When Jesus took on a human nature, as mentioned before, He made Himself subject to the same universal laws, absolutes, and Commandments that He, Himself, established as Creator. By entering the human race, Jesus indeed took a step down from His glory and splendor that He had prior to His Incarnation (**Philippians 2:5-11**). As a matter of fact, a careful reading of the words in the above text reveals this.

Jesus was telling His disciples that they should be happy that He will soon be returning to His Father because He will be returning to the glory that was His prior to the Incarnation (See **John Chapter 17**).

The concepts of God's Trinitarian nature and Jesus' Incarnation are difficult to grasp. Yet, the heart of Biblical Christianity will agree that we can not possibly expect to fully understand every aspect of the Creator and Sustainer of the vast universe because He is God; we are but mortal. It is, to the human mind and knowledge, impossible to understand fully how God can be human, omniscient, omnipresent and omnipotent; this is where faith is imperative. Similarly, it is unlikely that we are capable of understanding everything about God's nature as well since we are on a much lower level of understanding compared with God Himself. God's ways are beyond our ways, we simply can not fully comprehend God. Jesus came in the flesh to fully exegete God for man, (**John 1:18**). The word "exegete" simply means to reveal, to manifest, show forth. So, Jesus came in the flesh so man can see, experience, and have a relationship with God.

The Revelation of Muhammad On Trinity

God is the "Third Of Three"

It is the position of this author that Allah, as described in the Koran cannot possibly be equivalent to God of the Bible, as is claimed by Muslims. But, for the sake of simplicity, let's use Allah and God interchangeably as we read these Surahs from the Koran.

Surah 4:171 "O People of the Scripture (Christians)! Do not exceed the limits in your religion: Nor say of Allah aught but the truth. The Messiah (Jesus) the son of Mary was (no more than) a messenger of Allah, and His Word, which He bestowed on Mary, and a spirit proceeding from Him: so believe in Allah and His messengers. Say not "Three"(Trinity)! Cease! (it is better for you: for Allah is (the only) one god, Glory be to Him: (far exalted is He) above having a son. To Him belongs all that is in the heavens and all that is in the earth. And Allah is all sufficient as a Disposer of affairs."

Surah 5:73 "Surely disbelievers are those who said Allah is the third of the three (in a trinity). But there is no god (none who has the right to be worshipped) but one god, Allah. And if they cease not from what they say, verily a painful torment will befall on the disbelievers among them."

Surah 5:116 "And (remember) when Allah will say (on the Day of Resurrection): O (Jesus) son of Mary! Did you say to men: Worship me and my mother as two gods besides Allah? He will say: Glory be to you! It was not for me to say what I had no right (to say). Had I said such a thing, you would surely have known it. You know what is in my inner self though I do not know what is in yours. Truly, you and only you are the all-knower of all that is hidden (and unseen)."

Upon reading these passages, Muhammad's misconceptions of the Trinity are again clearly displayed. The attacks here are directed toward Christians and perhaps a heretical so-called Christian group, who, as perceived by Muhammad, practiced tri-theism rather than Trinitarian monotheism. It is implied here that other gods are worshiped besides Allah and that this is Trinitarian belief. **A book on Islam co-authored by a Christian apologist and a Muslim, claim that Allah and the God of the Bible are the same, just called different names.** With this belief in mind, it is understandable that the other two Members of the Trinity would be viewed as separate gods since only God the Father is Allah as believed by Islam. However, this perception is not accurate. Again, Christians teach that there is only one God that is comprised of three distinct, yet eternally unified, co-equal, equally powerful Persons, all three of whom have the same attributes of the Father. In other words, Christians believe that God the Father is God, Jesus is God, and the Holy Spirit is God – keeping in mind that "God" was properly used in the Old and New Testaments not as a proper noun, but as a "common noun" like deity. God, or Allah if we make the equivalence as the Muslims do, embodies all three Persons rather than just the Father, according to Christian beliefs. **So, the claim that Allah (or God) is the "third of three" is unfounded since Christians do not, nor**

have they ever, believed this. Christians would agree with Muslims that such a position would indeed be a blasphemous heresy as this describes, once again, tri-theism, not Trinitarian monotheism. <u>**Allah and God are not the same,**</u> **do not have the same attributes, and must be recognized and verbalized among Christians as different deities,** God the Father (**divine**); Allah, **deceptive** and **demonic**, a false god.

Jesus' Deity Rejected

Surah 5:73 "Surely disbelievers are thosee who said Allah is the third of the three (in a trinity). But there is no god (none who has the right to be worshipped) but one god, Allah. And if they cease not from what they say, verily a painful torment will befall on the disbelievers (non-Muslims) among them."

It may seem to be a matter of mere semantics, but necessary to comment on this particular passage. Christians do not claim that God was Jesus, but rather that Jesus is God, and did not exhaust or diminish God. Contrary to Koranic claims, Christians believe that Jesus, while representing the entire Godhead (**John 14:7-11, and 17**), is NOT the entire Godhead Himself. This passage makes it appear that, according to Christian beliefs, Jesus is Father, Son, and Holy Spirit yet Jesus is the fullness of the God-Head (**Colossians 2:9**). The Bible makes it clear, as discussed above, that Jesus, while being eternally unified with the Father, is a different Entity in His humanity within the Godhead as the Father. For example, Jesus would not have prayed to His Father if He was the Father.

Islamic theology as pictured and portrayed in the Koran serves a false god and should be fully rejected by every Christian. Christians must study the Word, preach and teach the Word, as well as defend the Word without any apology. The Koran and all it stands for and represents should be completely rejected as demonic and destructive.

THE KORAN SAYS THAT ISLAM CAME BEFORE JUDAISM AND CHRISTIANITY, IT WAS THE RELIGION PRACTICED BY ABRAHAM, YET THIS IS A BLATANT DEMONIC DECEPTION, A LIE CODIFIED IN THE KORAN.

13

Islam and THE JEWS

The hatred that exists today between Muslims and Jews is not just a modern phenomenon. Muhammad came into conflict with the Jewish tribes of his time, and this conflict ended in village raids, rape, looting, murder and subjection to Islam. Throughout the history of Islam Muhammad's anti-Jewish sentiments, codified in the *Koran* and *Hadith,* have caused hatred between Muslims and Jews. Today anti-Semitism reverberates throughout the Muslim world with an intensity not seen since the time of Hitler. Muhammad's own teachings in the Koran are used to justify it. Muslim children are taught that Jews are pigs and are hated by all of Islam. Even today in Muslim schools and universities children as well as adults are taught to kill Jews in Jihad. Regardless of what modern Islam claims, the real heart of Islam is to extinguish, annihilate all Jews on the face of the earth. The Islamic saying in the Middle East is to **"push all Jews into the great sea."** Today, the complete focus of Iran is on the ultimate destruction of Israel, and America because we stand with Israel.

Muhammad lived in seventh century A.D. At that time; the Jews had been worshiping Yahweh for almost twenty-five hundred years. Christians had been following Jesus for six hundred years and Muhammad had the opportunity to hear, and compare his Islamic teaching with Jewish and Christian teachings from God's word, The Bible.

Surah 29:46 " and argue not with the people of the scripture Jews and Christians unless it be in a way that is better (with good words and in good manner inviting them to Islamic monotheism with his verses) except with such of them as do wrong and say (to them) we believe in that which has been revealed to us and revealed to you, Allah and your God is one, and to him we have submitted (as Muslims)."

Surah 3:64 "say o Muhammad, o people of the scripture Jews and Christians come to a word that is just between us and you that we worship none but Allah (alone) and that we associate no partners either him and that none of us shall take others as lords as besides Allah then if turn away, say bear witness that we are Muslims."

How can this be? How could the prophets of the Bible be preaching Islam when the first time the world heard of Islam was through Muhammad's demonic

revelation? **The Koran says that Islam came before Judaism and Christianity, it was the religion practiced by Abraham, yet this is a blatant demonic deception, a lie codified in the Koran.**

Surah 3:67-68 "Ibrahim (Abraham) was neither a Jew nor a Christian but the true Muslim...verily, among mankind who have the best claim to Ibrahim (Abraham) are those who followed him and this prophet (Muhammad) and those who have believed (Muslims)."

The Koran refers to Islam as the religion of Abraham many times (Surah 2:130, 135, 3:95 4:125, 6:161). According to the Koran, Abraham and many prophets after him preached Islam, including Isaac, Ishmael, Jacob, Joseph, Noah, David Solomon, Moses John and Jesus (Surah 4:163; 6:84-86). This also is a lie from Satan recorded in his demonic book, the Koran.

When the Jewish leaders of Medina first heard of the coming of Muhammad and his teachings, they were inquisitive. They did not immediately accept or reject him, but they wanted to know more. Relations began to deteriorate as the Jews discovered Muhammad was ignorant of their scriptures and traditions. The rabbis would challenge him with questions that he could not answer. Thus, revealing Muhammad as a false prophet. Therefore, the Jews rejected Muhammad.

The Jews' rejection of Muhammad's message displeased him greatly. Although he was deceived, he believed he was verbalizing the same monotheism to which the Jews subscribed, why then wouldn't they accept him as a prophet? To establish his relationship with the Jews, he borrowed some Jewish practices and prescribed them to his followers.

Muslims were to meet for prayer on Friday afternoon as Jews prepare for the Sabbath, they were to face Jerusalem in prayer as Jews do, they were to observe some of the Jewish dietary laws, as well as the fast on the Day of Atonement. Muslims called this the fast of *Ashura,* meaning "tenth," since the Day of Atonement falls on the tenth of the Jewish month of Tishri.

The Jews rejected his revelations in spite of these practices, Muhammad changed them, and fixed the *qibla* (direction of prayer) to Mecca in place of Jerusalem. **Muhammad's new revelations thus canceled out Christianity and Judaism**. Read more about abrogation in chapter three. Islam teaches that Allah rejected the children of Israel because of their sins, and God went back to the seed of Abraham and chose a person from the line of Ishmael to be the final prophets **and Allah decreed that those who followed Muhammad's revelation would become the new chosen people**. Muhammad tried to re-write Biblical history to suit his need.

Surah 3:110 "You [true believers in Islamic monotheism, and real followers of prophet

Muhammad and his Sunnah] are the best of peoples ever raised up for mankind...had the people of the scripture, Jews and Christians believed it would have been better for them."

Surah 2:47 "o children of Israel remember my favor which I bestowed upon you and that I preferred you to the mankind and Jinn (of your time period, in the past)."

Allah Protected The Jews?

Surah 28:4-6 "Verily Fir'oun (pharaoh) exalted himself in the land and made its people sects, weakening (oppressing) a group (i.e. children of Israel) among them: killing their sons, and letting their females live. Verily, he was of the mufsidun (i.e. those who commit great sins and crimes, oppressors, tyrants). And we wished to do a favor to those who were weak (and oppressed) in the land, and to make them rulers and to make them the inheritors, and to establish them in the land, and we let Fir'aun (Pharaoh) and Haman and their hosts receive from them that which they feared."

Islam teaches that Muslims now have God's favor, not the Jews. But during the first half of his revelations, Muhammad received several favorable words about Jews. As he said "The Jews are Allah's only chosen people."

Muhammad presented these stories as so-called revelations to convince the Jews that their God was the

same as Allah (the Muslim god) of the Koran. These stories were meant to show that Allah remembered his chosen people and cared for them and wanted them to believe in Muhammad and to accept his revelations.

Allah Chose His Prophets from Jews

Surah 5:20 "And (remember) when Musa (Moses) said to his people, o my people: Remember the favor of Allah to you when he made prophets among you, made you kings and gave you what he had not given to any other......"

The Koran says that Allah honored Jewish people and chose all his prophets from them and made them kings and gives them riches.

Jews and Christians Who Believe in Allah

Surah 2:62 "Verily those who believe and those who are Jews and Christians and Sabiens whoever believes in Allah and the Last Day and does righteous good deeds shall have their reward with their Lord, on them shall be no fear, nor shall they grieve."

This Surah did not require Christians and Jews to accept Muhammad or Islam as the one true religion. It actually asked them only to do what they were already doing, believe in God referred to as Allah, believe in the last day or the Day of Judgment: Do good works. This Surah, an affirmation for Jews and Christians, was **simply a way to build a positive relationship between Muhammad and the**

other religions of the area that were worshiping one God, an attempt to encourage Jews to follow Muhammad. This tactic is still used today, as Muslims speak of Allah as the same God as found in the Bible, but Allah is a false, demonic god.

Jews and Christians who Follow the Bible

Surah 5:44 "Verily, we did send down the Taurat (Torah) to Musa (Moses) therein was guidance and light, by which the prophets, who submitted themselves to Allah's will, judged for the Jews."

Surah 5:66 " And if only they had acted according to the Torah, the Gospel and what has (now) been sent down to them (Koran) from their lord, they would surely have gotten provision from above them and from underneath their feet..."

The Koran is saying that Jews and Christians received their scriptures from God. If they applied their own scriptures to their lives, the Koran says that they would be happy.

Jews Want A Sign

The Jewish people have historically sought for signs (**1 Corinthians 1:18-25**). Therefore, they would ask Muhammad for signs to validate what he was saying. The Koran makes several references to this:

Surah 29:50 "And they say why are not signs sent down to him from his Lord?" These words are just like the Jews' words to Jesus six hundred years earlier (recorded in the New Testament).

John 2:18-19 "Then the Jews demanded of him what miraculous sign can you show us to prove your authority to do all this? Jesus answered them, destroy this temple, and I will raise it again in three days."

The Koran Answers the Challenge:

Surah 29:50-51 "And they say why are not signs sent down to him from his Lord? Say the signs are only with Allah, and I am only a plain Warner, is it not sufficient for them what we have sent down to you the book, (the Koran), which is recited to them..."

Muhammad was saying to the Jews, "I'm the prophet. Don't ask me for signs. They are for Allah to do and Allah said the Koran is sign enough for you."

Surah 20:133 "They say: why does he not bring us a sign (proof) from his Lord? Has there not come to them the proof of that which is (written) in the former papers (Scriptures, the Torah and the Gospel) about the coming of the prophet of the prophet Muhammad?

The Jews recognized Muhammad was not a real prophet. The Koran records that they started to make fun of him and of Islam and the Muslims.

Surah 3:181 "Indeed, Allah has heard the statement of those (Jews) who say truly Allah is poor and we are rich! We shall record what they have said and their killing of the prophets unjustly, and we shall say taste you the torment of the burning (fire)."

Surah 4:46 "Among these who are Jews, there are some who displace words from (their) right places and say, we hear your word (o Muhammad) and disobey and hear and let you (o Muhammad) hear nothing and with a twist of their tongues and as mockery of the religion (Islam)..."

After about a year in Medina, Muhammad had only converted a few Jews to Islam. The great majority of them rejected him completely, Muhammad has another revelation. The Koran comments;

Surah 4:46 "...Allah has cursed them for their disbelief so they believe not except a few."

Rejection of Muhammad

When the Jewish people decided that Muhammad was a fake, phony, false prophet not sent from God, they completely rejected him and his teachings. Then Muhammad received another so-called revelation from Allah. Each of Muhammad's revelations were in response to his being rejected as false, or to accomplish his own goals and desires of control and domination.

Surah 5:78 "Those among the children of Israel who disbelieved were cursed by the tongue of Dawud (David) and Isa (Jesus), son of Maryam (Mary). That was because they disobeyed (Allah and his messengers) and were ever transgressing beyond bounds."

Surah 2:47 "O Children of Israel! Remember my favor which I bestowed upon you and that I preferred you to the mankind and jinn (of your time period, in the past)." This earlier revelation said the Jews were Allah's chosen people.

Allah Judges Jews

Surah 7:166 "So when they (the Jews) exceeded the limits of what they were prohibited, we said to them: Be you monkeys, despised and rejected."

Surah 5:60 "Say (O Muhammad to the people of the Scripture) shall I inform you of something worse than that, regarding the recompense from Allah: those (Jews) who incurred the curse of Allah and his wrath and those of whom (some) he transformed into monkeys and swine's..."

Surah 2:65 "And indeed you knew those amongst you who transgressed in the matter of the Sabbath (i.e. Saturday). We said to them: be you monkeys despised and rejected."

Jews were Turned into Animals

Even today, Muslims degrade and dislike Jews because the Koran teaches that Jews are pigs and animals, not humans. Muslims are making decisions based on a demonic book.

Sahih Muslim 25:5389 "Allah messenger said do not greet the Jews and the Christians before they greet you and when you meet any one of them on the roads force them to go to the narrowest part of it."

Surah 5:70-71 "Verily, we took the covenant of the children of Israel and sent messengers to them. Whenever there came to them a messenger with what they themselves desired not, a group of them they called liars, and others among them they killed. They thought there would be no (trial or punishment) so they become blind and deaf..."

Surah 2:91 "And when it said to them (The Jews)...why then have you killed the prophets of Allah aforetime if you indeed have been believers?"

In Muhammad's revelations, he praised the Jews for being the source of all Allah's prophets. For Islam is the final religion and the Koran is the last testament therefore, Jews and Christians must be converted to Islam.

Surah 3:85 "And whoever seeks a religion other than Islam, it will never be accepted of him, and in the hereafter he will be one of the losers."

Jews Corrupted The Torah

In Islamic teaching, the Torah has been corrupted, therefore it is rejected and the Koran should be accepted. Muslims feel obligated to Allah to spread the Koranic revelation globally and cause all of the world to accept Islam or be killed via Jihad.

Surah 2:75 "...A party of them (Jewish rabbis) used to hear the word of Allah the Taurat (Torah), then they used to change it knowingly after they understood it."

Surah 5:13 "They (the Jews) change the words from their (right) places and have abandoned a good part of the message that was sent to them..."

Islam's Greatest Enemy—Jews

Surah 5:82 "Verily you find the strongest among men in enmity to the believers (Muslims) the Jews and those who are Al-mushrikun (idolaters, polytheists, disbelievers in the oneness of Allah, pagans)..."

Jews Hated Unless Converted To Islam

The only way for a Jew to be accepted in any sense would be to convert to Islam.

Surah 2:120 " Never will the Jews nor the Christians be pleased with you (o Muhammad) till you follow their religion..."

Jews The Cause of Wars

Islam teaches that all wars around the globe at anytime in history is because of the Jews. This is a major demonic belief in Islam.

Surah 5:64 "...We have put enmity and hatred amongst them (the Jews) till the day of resurrection. Every time they kindled the fire of war, Allah extinguished it, and they (ever) strive to make mischief on the earth..."

Koran Condemns Jews and Christians

Surah 5:18 "And (both) the Jews and the Christians say: we are the children of Allah and his loved ones. Say: why then does he punish you for your sins? Nay you are but human beings of those he has created..."

Thus, Muhammad's attempts to get Jews and Christians to convert to Islam failed. Therefore a "new" additional convenient revelation from a false "god," **Allah, came to justify the Islamic Jew-Christian hatred even today. The entire Muslim world hates the apple of God's eye (the Jews). Because America stands with Israel, the Muslims want to destroy America. May God grant America the wisdom and strength to continue standing with Israel.**

"...KILL THE PAGANS (NON-MUSLIMS) WHEREVER YOU FIND THEM..

SURAH 9:5 ."

14

Islam and **THE SWORD**

Today, Islam claims over 2 billion followers worldwide; it is rapidly growing in Europe, Africa and America. This movement is very aggressive and extremely violent; teaching that if someone will not willingly convert, that they must be brought to submission or eventually be eliminated via Jihad. This movement boldly demands the death of all who would oppose it. The name of the movement, religion, ideology is "Islam." It invaded our shores under the protection of our freedom of religion, and is spreading in every direction thanks to our socialist media, taking advantage of people's lack of knowledge of the Arabic language and Islamic history. Islam, however, is more than a religion; it is a comprehensive way of life. Islam has religious, legal, political, economic, social and military components. The religious component is controller of all others. Those who defend Islam claim that Muslims desire to live peacefully with all men, **yet the facts of history prove that if and when Muslims gain control they will fight and even kill in order to eliminate all opposition to Islam,**

usually this aggressive aspect will begin to surface with only a three to ten percent Muslim population in a nation.

The Koran and the Hadith; the Muslim's holy books, contain the religious, social, civil, commercial, military, political and legal codes for all Islam. What many people do not realize is that the teachings of Islam are not just so-called ethical guidelines; they are binding laws with severe punishments attached to them that range from public whipping to chopping off of body parts and beheading. In the hands of Muslims, this type of law (sharia law), once established, inevitably leads to gross abuse and oppression of all non-Muslims. As in most countries where the Islamic code of law is enforced, the average citizen suffers while the crimes and hypocrisy of the Islamic leaders and those in power go unpunished. Christians and Jews are abused, accused and are shut off from any legal protection. Today, Christians and churches are destroyed, yet the demonic Islamic authorities are looking the other way. All we need to do is look at not just Islamic nations, but France, Germany, Russia, The Netherlands, Israel and Africa to see the terror, the dismemberment and death that brings the silence of fear upon its citizens.

A Religion of The Sword

The most alarming thing about Islam is that when it becomes powerful enough, the option for those under its control wouldn't be whether to accept Islam or reject it. It would be, rather, whether to accept Islam or, at best, become second class citizens, **at worst face DEATH**. Allah's instructions are clear:

Surah 9:5 "...Kill the pagans (non-Muslims) wherever you find them..."

According to the Koran there shouldn't be another religion besides Islam in any part of the world.

"The size and nature of Britain's Muslim population presents a threat to national security."

Professor David Voas
Manchester University

Surah 3:85 "And whoever seeks a religion other than Islam, never will it be accepted of him; and in the hereafter he will be one of the losers."

Some suggest that Islam speaks well about "People of the Book" (Christians and Jews). Well, not so. Read on:

A History of Terrorism

Muslims have been using the power of terror throughout history, following Allah's instructions on how to deal with the infidels (non-Muslims). The prophet of Islam himself engaged in many military battles and was merciless to his enemies, even these who simply attacked him verbally. His original sympathies with Jews and Christians as peoples of the book give way to a harsher treatment **when they did not follow Islam**. In one infamous episode, Muhammad cut the hands off hundreds of Jewish males of the Banu Qurayza tribe who did not side with him in battle. Muhammad is quoted as saying, "**the sword is the key of heaven and hell: a drop of blood shed in the cause of Allah, a night spent in arms, is of more avail than two months of fasting or fasting and prayer: whosoever falls in battle (jihad), his sins are forgiven, and at the day of Judgment his limbs shall be supplied by the wings of angels and cherubim.**"

Surah 8:60 *"And make against them all you can of power, including steeds of war (tanks, planes, missiles, artillery) to threaten the enemy of Allah and your enemy..."*

This Surah fits well with other Koranic Surahs in which Jihad means personal and communal spiritual struggle or striving. But the Koran for the most part uses Jihad to mean holy war and the language is extreme, and expressly clear. The symbol of Islam is the crescent, star and sword. The march toward global control is evident today.

Surah 5:33 "The punishment of these who wage war against Allah and his messenger, and do mischief in the land is only that they shall be killed or crucified or their hands and their feet be cut off from opposite sides, or be exiled from the land. That is their disgrace in this world, and a heavy punishment is theirs in the hereafter."

Both the example of the prophet and some emphasis in the Koran provided authorization for Islam's earliest leaders to spread Islam by military battle and conquest. **Bloody expansionism was also justified through original Islamic**

law that divided the world into two realms Dar al-Herb (**the land of war**) and Dar al-Islam (**land under Islamic rule**). Islam in any nation is <u>at all times in one of the stages</u>, <u>either at war or in control</u>.

Surah 2:216 "Jihad (holy fighting in Allah's cause) is ordained for you (Muslims) though you dislike it, and it may be that you dislike a thing which is good for you and that you like a thing which is bad for you. Allah knows but you do not know."

Surah 9:5 "Then when the sacred months are past, then kill the **pagans** (non-Muslims) wherever you find them, and capture them **and beseige them**, and lie in wait for them in each and every ambush. But if they repent, and establish regular prayers and practice regular charity then leave their way free. Verily, Allah is oft-forgiving, most merciful".

Surah 9:29 "fight those who (**1**) believe not in Allah, (**2**) nor the last day, (**3**) nor forbid that which has been forbidden by Allah and his messenger, (**4**) and those who acknowledge not the religion of truth (i.e. Islam) among the people of the Scripture (Christians and Jews) until they pay the Jizyah taxes with willing submission, and feel themselves subdued."

These two Surahs are known as "the verse of the sword," for this, a view of Jihad, until modern times and **all Muslims using this verse which commanded them to slay**

the pagans and the people of the book (Jews and Christians).

No matter how many people say Islam is religion of peace and Muhammad is prophet of Allah; **Muhammad was not only a religious leader, but a blood-thirsty, power-hungry, military leader who waged war against his enemies as soon as he had the means.** Therefore, Islam "<u>is not a religion of peace</u>." Muslims follow not only the Koran, which they believe is a literal transcript of Allah's words, as given to Muhammad, but also the Hadith, which are accounts of Muhammad's musings, sayings and works. These words and deeds are considered inspired by Allah and are edicts and directives, literally commands for Muslims to obey, even today Muslims that acknowledge the Koran are in fact followers of and believers in **the Sword, Jihad and the domination of the world by Islam**. Almost daily you read or view on TV about another act of Islamic Jihad, not just 9-11, but Fort Hood, as well as hundreds of other acts of Jihad attempted, such as the Times Square bomber, the shoe bomber, et al. The sad thing is that our national law enforcement and national security agencies are not informing the citizens that these attempts of terrorism are "<u>**all Islamic**</u>."

According to statistical facts, once a nation gets between a three and ten percent Muslim population, <u>**the Islamists will begin to push for the following**</u>:

• The introduction of "halal"(clean by Islamic standards) food.

- Pressuring supermarket chains to stock "halal" foods.

- Begin to push to get the government to allow them to rule themselves under "sharia," Islamic law.

- Begin to say that any "non-Muslim action" will offend the Muslims (cartoons, roadway signs about Islam, news articles, speeches, etc.) resulting in car burnings, political threats, instigation of false claims to get F.B.I. and law enforcement to investigate the "false claims."

- Start seeking governmental appointments or positions of authority.

- Start a major increase of building of mosques, over 3,000 in America today.

- Ultimately, they will demand the right to broadcast their 5 times a day prayers for all to hear. This is now happening in several places in Michigan.

- Rioting, jihad missions, killings, burning of Christian churches and Jewish Synagogues.

All of this under the banner of "<u>peaceful Islam</u>." Even when Islam is 100% in a nation like Afghanistan, Saudi Arabia, Somalia, Yemen, etc. There is "**no peace**."

It is the opinion of this author that America must wake up; we are seeing all of these signs NOW. We must elect patriots and place them in office that understand Islam and will pledge to protect us from Islamic demands and dominance. We must consider the fact that, based on the Muslim birth rate, Islam will exceed 50% of the whole population by the year 2050 according to demographic studies.

Islam is evil, very evil, wicked; started by a self-appointed prophet, a demon–possessed pedophile that justified the most wicked acts of terrorism and brutality the world has ever known.

"„„ADMONISH THEM FIRST, NEXT REFUSE TO SHARE THEIR BEDS (AND LAST) BEAT THEM..."

SURAH 4:34

15

Islam and WOMEN

In Islam, women are second-class citizens, just property. This is the result of both the Koran and other Islamic teachings, like the Hadith. The Koran has a great deal to say about the status of women in society and the treatment of women. Some of the Koran deals with marriage and divorce, modesty, and inheritance. Many of the passages are quite explicit, while others are a little more difficult to understand when examined by the western mind. The Koranic passages are very important because Muslims believe that the Koran is the literal word of Allah given to Muhammad by Gabriel. Therefore, Muslims do not believe that these passages can be questioned and should be believed and practiced in the Islamic legal code (i.e. Sharia Law) without question. In fact, Islamic religious teachers and scholars already practice the Koranic teachings in Muslim households in America, and are pushing for Sharia Law in the U.S.A. Because so many of the Koranic passages are very specific and clear, thus there is no way of questioning them or their interpretation, the text speaks for itself.

165

Women are simply powerless within Islam. Women are treated as furniture and face persecution without any sense or hope of rescue. Women are left helpless and hopelessly locked in a religious system of ideology that will ultimately destroy them, yet, Muslim leaders around the world refute the proof as seen in Muslim women's lives.

Many Koranic Surahs relate to topics concerning women. Some are clearly written and require no interpretation and others are less clear. It is the intent of this chapter to try to shed some light on these passages as well as further reveal the reality of the extreme dangers of the Koran and its teachings from which over one and a half billion Muslims follow daily.

Marriage and Divorce

Surah 2:221 "And do not marry idolatresses til they believe (Worship Allah alone). And indeed a slave woman who believes is better than a (free) idolatress, even though she pleases you. And give not your daughters in marriage to (idolatrous men), til they believe in Allah alone, and verily a believing slave is better than a (free) idolater, even though he pleases you Those idolators invite you to the Fire, but Allah invites (you) to Paradise and forgiveness by his leave and makes his (proofs, evidences, verses, lessons, signs, revelations, etc.) clear to mankind that they may remember."

Surah 2:229 "The divorce is twice, after that, either you retain her on reasonable terms or release her with kindness. And it is not lawful for you (men) to take back (from your wives) any of your (bridal money given by the husband to his wife at the time of marriage)..."

Surah 2:230 "And if he has divorced her (the third time), then she is not lawful unto him thereafter until she has married another husband. Then if he (the other husband) divorces her it is no sin for both of them that they reunite again if they feel that they can keep the limits ordained by Allah.... "

Surah 4:3 "And if you fear that you shall not be able to deal justly with the orphangirls then marry (other) women of your choice, two or three or four; but if you fear that you will not be able to deal justly (with them) then only one or (the slaves) that your right hands possess; That is nearer to prevent you from doing injustice." Another translation reads, "If you deem it best for the orphans, you may marry their mothers you may marry two, three, or four. If you fear lest you become unfair, then you shall be content with only one, or with what you already have. Additionally, you are thus more likely to avoid financial hardship."

Polygamy is Approved

Surah 4:21 "And how could you take it (back), while you have gone in unto each other, and they have taken from you a firm and strong covenant?"

Surah 4:22 "And marry not women whom your fathers married, except what has already passed; indeed it was shameful and most hateful, and an evil way."

Surah 4:23 "Prohibited to you (for marriage) are: your mothers, your daughters, your sisters, your father's sisters, your mother's sisters, your brother's daughters, your sister's daughters, your foster mothers who gave you suck, your foster milk suckling sisters, your wives' mothers, the stepdaughters under your guardianship, born of your wives to who you have gone in—but there is no sin if you have not gone in them (to marry their daughters)—the wives of your sons who (spring) from your own loins, and two sisters in wedlock at the same time—except for what has already passed; verily, Allah is oft-forgiving, most merciful."

Surah 4:24 "Also (forbidden are) women who are already married, except those slaves whom your right hands possess. Thus Allah has ordained for you. All others are lawful, provided you seek (them in marriage), with Mahr (bridal money given by the husband to his wife at the time of marriage) from your property, desiring chastity, not committing illegal sexual intercourse, so with those of whom you have enjoyed sexual relations, give them their Mahr as prescribed; but if after a Mahr is prescribed, you agree mutually (to give more), there is no sin on you. Surely, Allah is ever all knowing, all-wise." (See 60:10.)

Surah 4:25 "And whoever of you have not the means wherewith to wed free, believing women, they may wed believing girls from among those (slaves) whom your right hands possess, and Allah has full knowledge about your faith, you are one from another. Wed them with the permission of their own folk (guardians, or masters) and give them their Mahr according to what is reasonable; they (the above said captive slave girls) should be chaste, not committing illegal sex, nor taking boy-friends. And after they have been taken in wedlock, if they commit illegal sexual intercourse, their punishment is half that for free (unmarried) women. This is for him among you who is afraid of being harmed in his religion or in his body; but it is better for you if you practice self-restraint, and Allah is oft-forgiving, most merciful."

Women are Inferior to Men

Surah 4:34 "Men are the protectors and maintainers of women, because Allah has made one of them to excel the other, and because they spend (to support them) from their means. Therefore the righteous women are devoutly obedient (to Allah and their husbands), and guard in the husband's absence what Allah orders them to guard, (e.g. their chastity, their property.) As to those women on whose part you see ill-conduct, admonish them (first), (next), refuse to share their beds, (and last) <u>beat them (lightly if it is useful</u>); but if they return to obedience, seek not against them means (of annoyance). Surely Allah is ever most high, most great."

Surah 4:128 "If a wife fears cruelty or desertion on her husband's part, there is no sin on them both if they make terms of peace between themselves; and making peace is better. And human inner-selves are swayed by greed... "

Surah 4:129 "You will never be able to do perfect justice between wives, even if it is your ardent desire, so do not incline too much to one of them (by giving her more of your time and provision) so as to leave the other hanging (i.e. neither divorced nor married).. And if you do justice, and do all that is right and fear Allah by keeping away from what is wrong, then Allah is ever oft-Forgiving, Most Merciful."

This Surah requires a man to deal justly, both materially and emotionally, with "all" of his wives. It insightfully points out that this is not possible. A few Muslim nations have used this contradiction to justify the banning of polygamy. This is not a logic that appeals to most Islamics because this would admit that there are contradictions within the Koran and therefore Allah was confused, and the Koran is in error, therefore not trustworthy.

Surah 5:5 "Made lawful for you this day are [all kinds of lawful foods, which Allah has made lawful (meat of slaughtered eatable animals, milk products, fats, vegetables and fruits.

The food (slaughtered cattle, eatable animals of the people of the Scripture (Christians and Jews) is lawful to you and yours is lawful to them. (Lawful to you in marriage) are chaste women from the believers and chaste women from those who were given the Scripture (Jews and Christians) before your time, when you have given their due Mahr...You shall maintain chastity, not committing adultery, nor taking girl-friends. Anyone who rejects faith, all his work will be in vain, and in the Hereafter he will be with the losers."

Surah 24:32 "And marry those among you who are single (i.e.a man who has no wife and a woman that has no husband) and (also marry) the (pious, fit and capable ones) of your (male) slaves and maid-servants (female slaves). If they be poor, Allah will enrich them out of his bounty. And Allah is all-sufficient for his creatures' needs, all-knowing (about the state of the people)."

Surah 25:74 "And those who say, "Our Lord! Bestow on us from our wives and our offspring the comfort of our eyes, and make us leaders of the pious."

Surah 30:21 "Among His signs is this, that He created for you wives from among yourselves, that you may find repose in them, and He has put between you affection and mercy. Verily, in that are indeed signs for a people who reflect."

Surah 40:8 "Our Lord! And make them enter the (Eden) Paradise (everlasting gardens) which You have promised them--and to be righteous among their fathers, their wives, and their offspring! Verily, You are the All-mighty, the All-Wise."

Wife-Beating Permitted

Surah 4:34 "...As to those women on whose part you see ill-conduct, admonish them (first), (next), refuse to share their beds, (and last) beat them (lightly if it is useful); but if they return to obedience, seek not against them means (of annoyance). Surely Allah is ever most high, most great."

This passage has been debated by Islamic scholars. Some Islamics accept the translation **"beat them."** Others maintain that there are alternative translations, including **"turn away from them,"** **"go along with them,"** and perhaps even, **"have consensual sex with them"**. Most traditional Muslims insist on the first translations, (beat them). Muslims can not openly or overtly challenge the Koran, thus the only way to bring a modern (western-world) acceptance of how husbands should treat their wives is to feign a challenge of the translation. It is notable that many of the groups and individuals in the Muslim world that today advocate Sharia Law prefer the more severe interpretations of the Koran such as the reference to beating women; here are the references to amputations and other severe punishments in other Koranic Surahs.

Beating of Women in Islam

Some translations of the Koran have tried to suggest that the word "beat" means to hit softly. However, the same Arabic word is used in Surah 8:12 which reads:

Surah 8:12 "(Remember) when your lord revealed to the angels; Verily, I am with you so keep firm those who have believed. I will cast terror into the hearts of those who have disbelieved, so **strike** them over the necks, and **smite** off all their fingers and toes."

Abu Dawud 693 "Umar reported the Prophet as saying, A man will not be asked about why he beat his wife."

Muslim 5:690 "Umar then came forward, and when he had asked and had been granted permission, he found the Prophet sitting sad and silent with his wives around him. He told that he decided to say something which would make the Prophet laugh, so he said, "Messenger of Allah, I wish you had seen the daughter of Kharija when she asked me for extra money and I got up and slapped her on the neck." God's messenger laughed and said, "They are around me as you see asking for extra money." Abu Bakr then got up, went to A'isha and slapped her on the neck, and Umar did the same to Hafsa. (Mishkat Al-Masabih, p. 690: Muslim)

Abu Dawud 692 "Iyas b. Abdullah reported God's messenger as saying, "Do not beat Allah 's handmaidens" but when Umar came to God's messenger and said, The women have become emboldened towards their husbands", he gave license to beat them. Then many women went round god's messenger's family complaining of their husbands. Those are not the best among you."

In October, 2010, a New Jersey Court ruled spousal abuse acceptable under Islam. This judge held that the defendant could not be held responsible for the violent sexual assaults of his wife because he did not have the specific intent to sexually assault his wife, and because his actions were "consistent with his [religious] practices." In other words, the judge refused to issue the permanent restraining order because under Sharia Law, this Muslim husband had a "right" to rape and beat his wife.

Muhammad Beat His Wives

Muslim 4:2127 "He (Muhammad b. Qais) then reported that it was 'A'isha who had narrated this: Should I not narrate to you about myself and about the Messenger of Allah (may peace be upon him)? We said: Yes. She said: When it was my turn for Allah's Messenger (may peace be upon him) to spend the night with me, he turned his side, put on his mantle and took off his shoes and placed them near his feet, and spread the corner of his shawl on his bed and then lay down till he thought that I had gone to sleep. He took hold of his mantle slowly and put on the shoes slowly, and opened the door and went out and then closed it lightly. I

174

covered my head, put on my veil and
tightened my waist wrapper, and then went
out following his steps till he reached Baqi'.
He stood there and he stood for a long time.
He then lifted his hands three times, and
then returned and I also returned. He
hastened his steps and I also hastened my
steps. He ran and I too ran. He came (to the
house) and I also came (to the house). I,
however, preceded him and I entered (the
house), and as I lay down in the bed, he (the
Holy Prophet) entered the (house), and said:
Why is it, O 'A'isha, that you are out of
breath? I said: There is nothing. He said:
Tell me or the Subtle and the Aware would
inform me. I said: Messenger of Allah, may
my father and mother be ransom for you,
and then I told him (the whole story). He
said: Was it the darkness (of your shadow)
that I saw in front of me? I said: Yes. **He
struck me on the chest which caused me
pain**, and then said: 'Did you think that
Allah and His Apostle would deal unjustly?'

Women and Oppression

Surah 4:15 "And those of your women who
commit illegal sexual intercourse, take the
evidence of four witnesses from amongst
you against them; and if they testify, <u>confine
them (i.e. women) to houses until death
comes to them</u> of Allah ordains another
way."

**Islamic women live lives of mere existence and
repression as seen in the required coverings called**

burquas. The requirement to wear burquas is perhaps the most demeaning treatment of Muslim women.

Surah 24:31 "And tell the believing women to lower their gaze (from looking at forbidden things), and protect their private parts (from illegal sexual acts) and not to show off their adornments except only that which is apparent (like both eyes for necessity to see the way, or outer palms of hands or one eye or dress like veil, gloves, head-cover, apron, etc.) and to draw their veils all of (i.e. their bodies, faces, necks and bosoms) and not to reveal their adornment except to their husbands, their fathers, or their sons, or their husband's fathers, or their sons, or their brothers or their brother's sons, or their sister's sons, or their (Muslim) women (i.e. sisters in Islam), or the female slaves whom their right hands possess, or old male servants who lack vigor, or small children who have no sense of feminine sex. And let them not stamp their feet so as to reveal what they hide of their adornment, and all of you beg Allah to forgive you all, O believers, that you may be successful."

Surah 4:11 "Allah commands you as regards your children's (inheritance): <u>to the male a portion equal to that of two females</u>..."

This Surah is widely used throughout the Muslim world to set the inheritance of daughters as that of half of brothers. The Koranic provision is carefully followed in traditional Muslim societies and families. This Surah is very clearly written and there is little Muslims can do to reinterpret the passage. The problem of trying to modify or change this Koranic Surah is very clear and advocating change in the eyes of Islamics is advocating changing the very law of Allah. This passage dehumanizes the value of women to half the value of a man.

Surah 4:12 "In what your wives leave, your share is a half, if they have no child; but if they leave a child, you get a fourth of that which they leave after payment of legacies that you may have bequeathed or debts. In that which you leave, their (your wives) share is a fourth, if you leave no child; but if you leave a child, they get an eighth of that which you leave; after payment of legacies that you may have bequeathed or debts...."

The Husband's Sexual Desires

The Koran, speaking figuratively about sex, says of women:

Surah 2:223 "Your wives are a tilth for you, so go to your tilth, when or how you will..."

Muhammad gave strong warnings to women who would not accommodate their husbands/masters desire.

Bukhari 7:121 "Narrated Abu Huraira: The Prophet said, if a man invites his wife to sleep with him an she refuses to come to him, then angels send their curses on her till morning."

The Koran gives permission to the Muslim man to literally rape his wife should he desire to do so.

Muslim Men's Reward

Surah 44:51-54 "Verily the pious will be in place of security (Paradise). Among gardens and springs, dressed in fine silk and (also) in thick silk, facing each other, So, it (will be). And shall marry them to (fair females) with wide, lovely eyes."

Surah 78:31-33 "Verily, for the pious there will be a success (Paradise); gardens and vineyards, and young full-breasted (mature) maidens of equal age..."

Surah 56:34-35 "And on couches or thrones raised high. Verily we have created them (maidens) of special creation."

One reported Allah 's messenger as saying that no woman annoys her husband in this world without his wife among the large-eyed maidens saying, "You must not annoy him. Allah curse you! He is only a passing guest with you and is about to leave you to come to us."

Mental Capacity of Women

The Koran says that the testimony of a <u>woman is not equal to that of a man</u>. It says that the testimony of two women is required to be equal to the testimony of one man. In Islam, women have <u>no voice</u>, <u>no value</u> and <u>no validation</u>; they are just "things." A Muslim woman's testimony is worth only half that of a man.

Surah 2:282 "...And get two witnesses out of your own men. And if there are not two men (available), then a man and two women, such as you agree for witnesses, so that if one of them (two women) errs, the other can remind her..."

Why is it that the testimony of a woman is only worth half that of a man? Muhammad explains in the following hadith.

Bukhari 3:826 "Narrated Abu Said Al-Khudri: The Prophet said, "Isn't the witness of a women equal to half that of a man?" The women said "yes." He said "This is because of the deficiency of a woman's mind."

More Women than Men in Hell

Just a few readings in the Hadith say:

Muslam 4:6597 "Ibn Abbas reported that Allah's Messenger said: I had a chance to look into paradise and I found that majority of the people was poor and I looked into the Fire and there I found the majority constituted by women.

Muslam 4:6600 "Imran b. Husain reported that Allah's Messenger said: Amongst the inmates of Paradise the women would form a minority."

Covering and Women in Islam

Surah 33:59 "O Prophet, tell your wives and your daughters and the women of the believers to draw their cloaks (veils) all over their bodies (i.e. screen themselves completely except for the eyes or one eye to see the way). That will be better that they should be known (as free respectable women) so as not to be annoyed."

Surah 24:31 "And tell the believing women to lower their gaze (from looking at forbidden things), and protect their private parts (from illegal sexual acts) and not to show off their adornments except only that which is apparent (like both eyes for necessity to see the way, or outer palms of hands or one eye or dress like veil, gloves, head-cover, apron, etc.) and to draw their veils all of (i.e. their bodies, faces, necks and bosoms) and not to reveal their adornment except to their husbands, their fathers, or their sons, or their husband's fathers, or their sons, or their brothers or their brother's sons, or their sister's sons, or their (Muslim) women (i.e. sisters in Islam), or the female slaves whom their right hands possess, or old male servants who lack vigor, or small children who have no sense of feminine sex. And let them not stamp their feet so as to reveal what they hide of their adornment, and all of you beg Allah to forgive you all, O believers, that you may be successful."

The woman is not only supposed to cover herself, except with relatives, but to look down, so as to avoid making eye-contact with men. This is the reason most Muslim women wear the full black body coverings called burquas. This is the ultimate of oppression and degrading of Islamic women. One must ask the question, "**Why would any woman want to be Muslim**?"

Bukhari 1:321 "...Muhammad is asked whether it is right for a young woman to leave her house without a veil. He replies, *"She should cover herself with the veil of her companion."*

Bukhari 6:282 Narrated Safuya bint Shaiba, "Aisha used to say when the verse: (Surah 24:31) 'they should draw their veils over their necks and bosoms' was revealed, (the ladies) cut their waist sheets at the edges and covered their faces with the cut pieces."

Abu Dawud (2:641) " The Prophet (peace be upon him) said: <u>Allah does not accept the prayer of a woman</u> who has reached puberty <u>unless she wears a veil.</u>"

Bukhari 4:250 Narrated Ibn Abbas"[The Prophet said] "It is not permissible for a man to be alone with a woman, and no lady should travel except with a Muhram (i.e. her husband or a person whom she cannot marry in any case for ever; e.g. her father, brother, etc.)." - Neither is a woman allowed to travel by herself."

Islamic law (Sharia) clearly requires women to cover themselves. The degree of covering varies with how seriously a Muslim government interprets this, with the Taliban's Afghanistan at one extreme (requiring full burquas) and moderate governments such as Turkey and Tunisia (actually banning headscarves in public buildings) at the other. Most Islamic religious leaders advocate full sharia law and full compliance with the Koran, which would require full body coverings. This is seen all over Europe and more and more in America. There is a movement in America to allow Muslims to establish Sharia Law for the Muslims in the U.S. In March 2011, a Tampa, FL Judge used Sharia Law to rule in a case involving Muslims.

The head covering is interpreted as a symbol of <u>male domination</u> by some outside the faith, and by many Muslim women in western nations, who have been fighting for the right to dress as they please. In December of 2007, a father in Canada beat his 16 year-old daughter to death for refusing to wear the hijab (headscarf).

"AND IF YOU FEAR THAT YOU SHALL NOT BE ABLE TO DEAL JUSTLY WITH THE ORPHAN-GIRLS, THEN MARRY (OTHER) WOMEN OF YOUR CHOICE, TWO THREE OR FOUR; BUT IF YOU FEAR THAT YOU SHALL NOT BE ABLE TO DEAL JUSTLY (WITH THEM), THEN ONLY ONE OR (THE SLAVES) THAT YOUR RIGHT HANDS POSSESS. THAT IS NEARER TO PREVENT YOU FROM DOING INJUSTICE."

SURAH 4:3

16

Islam and **POLYGAMY**

According to Islam, the Koran is the final authority to all the world, so its teaching should spread around the globe for the good of humanity. However, one of its clear teachings says that men may be polygamous. Dr. Lois Lamya' al Faruqi, a Muslim feminist, says in her work, "**Confrontation or Cooperation**," that polygamy, which she has renamed 'polygyny,' poses no threat to society because it is used only in extraordinary circumstances. This is simply a technical turn on words to authorize multiple sexual encounters for Muslim men, yet striving to follow the Koran.

> *"Muslims view polygyny as an institution which is to be called into use only under extraordinary circumstances. As such, it has not been generally regarded by Muslim women as a threat. Attempts by the feminist movement to focus on eradication of this institution in order to improve the status of women would therefore meet with little sympathy or support."*

However, in normal usage "polygyny" is worse than polygamy because it denotes sexual liaisons without marriage. But her article seeks to protect the Koran on this issue without eliminating the practice—having your cake and eating it too. The average western rational mind, especially in America, the practice is viewed as clearly wrong and immoral. Dr. Lamya' al Faruqi continues:

> *"There are some men who may have strong physical desires, for whom one wife is not enough. If the door is closed to such a man and he is told, you are not allowed more than one wife, this will cause great hardship to him, and his desire may find outlets in forbidden ways."*

Rather than realizing that this should be called sin to be forsaken, there is an attempt to further authorize it based on a book that is "un-holy," the Koran.

Maximum of Four Wives

Surah 4:3 "And if you fear that you shall not be able to deal justly with the orphan-girls, then marry (other) women of your choice, two three or four; but if you fear that you shall not be able to deal justly (with them), then only one or (the slaves) that your right hands possess. That is nearer to prevent you from doing injustice."

Surah 66:5 "It may be if he divorced you (all) that his Lord will give him instead of you, wives better than you-Muslims (who submit to Allah)…"

Bukhari 1:268 Narrated Qatada: "Anas bin Malik said, The Prophet used to visit all his wives in a round, during the day and night and they were eleven in number." I asked Anas, "Had the Prophet the strength for it?" Anas replied, "We used to say that the Prophet was given the strength of thirty men." Muhammad had special rules that allowed him at least eleven wives. (His successors had more than four wives at a time as well.)

Bukhari 7:6 "The Prophet used to go round (have sexual relations with) all his wives in one night, and he had nine wives."

Bukhari 8:598 "Allah's Apostle said, "No woman should ask for the divorce of her sister (Muslim) so as to take her place, but she should marry the man (without compelling him to divorce his other wife).

Without question, polygamy in the Koran is firmly stated and accepted in Islam. One of the ridiculous arguments used in defense of polygamy with Islam is that it reduces prostitution by satisfying a man's sexual desires in a way that one woman cannot. America be warned, should we allow Sharia Law for Islam, America will face the legalization of polygamy.

The same Koranic Surah also gives a man license to capture women and use them as sex slaves but is simply overlooked by Islam's apologists. But polygamy was practiced in Arabia for different reasons also.

Islamic Practices

First, it is said that in pre-Islamic Arabia, guardian men married the orphan girls under their care, so the Koran says that they should direct their attention to women other than the orphans.

Second, in pre-Islamic days men used to marry a limitless number of women and grab the property of their orphan nephews and nieces to support their wives.

Third, in pre-Islamic days, men could marry as many women as they wanted and "treat them cruelly and unjustly" with impunity. Therefore, the Koran limits the number to four, and only if the man could take care of them all: "But if you realize that you might not be able to do justice to them."

Also, the clause **"marry those who have fallen in your possession"** means slave-girls who were captured in a war. Men may "marry" them because slaves do not require as much expense, not as much cost of free women.

The paraphrases of this clause could simply be, "If you need more than one [wife] but are fearful that you might not be able to afford your wives from among the free people, you may then seek slave girls because in this event you will have less responsibility. This is not surprising, **because the slave-girl was considered sexual property.**

Surah 4:24 "Also (forbidden are) women already married, except those (slaves) whom your right hands possess. Thus has Allah ordained for you. All others are lawful provided you seek (them in marriage) with mahr (bridal money given by the husband to his wife at the time of marriage) from your property desiring chastity, not committing illegal sexual intercourse, so with those of whom you have enjoyed sexual relations, give them their mahr as prescribed but if after a mahr is prescribed, you agree mutually (to give more), there is no sin on you. Surely, Allah is ever All-knowing, All-wise."

Therefore, the so-called **limit of only four wives is an artificial limit.** **Muslim men could have sex with as many women as they wanted from among their slaves.** The Koran is a total contradiction to all the Bible teaches. It is so ironic, a Muslim man will reject alcoholic beverages, or eating pork, yet find nothing wrong with illegal drugs or sexual dissipation.

Temporary Wives

In Shiite Islam, which is the dominant form of Islam in Iran, there is an allowance for **"temporary" wives.** This provision allows men to have female companionship on a short term basis. Couples could sign an agreement for a period of time as brief as three nights.

It is clear that this is done to be able to say that the sexual relationship was in marriage. Nothing more than an attempt to cover known sin.

Special Marriage Privileges

Allah gave Muhammad special permission to marry as many women as he desired or take them as slaves or concubines. By his own example and life, he seemed to perpetuate these practices. It seems that Allah grants Muhammad wide latitude in his marriages. Whatever Muhammad wanted to do, he would have another revelation from Allah that would authorize his desires.

Surah 33:50 "O Prophet (Muhammad)! We have made lawful to you your wives, to whom you have paid mahr (bridal money given by the husband to his wife at the time of marriage), and those (slaves) whom your right hand possesses-whom Allah has given to you, and the daughters of your (paternal and maternal uncles) and the daughters of your (paternal and maternal aunts), who have migrated (from Mecca) with you, and a believing woman if she offers herself to the *Prophet, and if the Prophet wants to marry her-a privilege for you only, not for the (rest of) the believers..."*

Surah 23:5-6 "And those who guard their chastity, (i.e. private parts from illegal sexual acts) except their wives or (the slaves) that their right hands possess-for then they are free from blame..."

Surah 23 was revealed during the prophet's life in Mecca before his Hijrah or Emigration from his home city to Medina in A.D. 622. During the early years of his

journey, he never waged war on anyone, so these were times of peace. These times were however limited, and lasted only until he could garner strength in followers. Islam's ploy has always been "peace" while small, but wage war when size and strength according to number would allow war and victory.

The key words are "those who are legally in their possession," (Surah 23:56), Maududi (d. 1979) is a highly respected commentator on the Koran, and he interprets the plain meaning of the clause, saying that sex with slave-girls is lawful for Muslims.

Maududi writes: 7:241 *"Two categories of women have been excluded from the area legally in one's possession, i.e. slave-girls. Thus the verse clearly lays down the law that one is allowed to have sexual relation with one's slave-girl as with one's wife, the basis being possession and not marriage. If marriage had been the condition, the slave-girl also would have been included among the wives, and there was no need to mention them separately."*

The main point in this section, which Maududi overlooks or refuses to criticize; is that Muhammad himself endorses not only the entire institution of slavery, but also sex between male owners and their female slaves within this institution. One cannot criticize Muhammad without seriously damaging Islam. Any criticism of Muhammad is viewed as blasphemy and punishable by death.

Sex With Slave-Girls

After Muhammad left Mecca and now in Medina, Surah 4 is said to have been revealed to him. Muhammad continues his policy of sex between male owners and their female slaves in Medina, with an added twist of enslaving women prisoners of war and permitting his soldiers to have sex with them.

Surah 4:24 *"Also (forbidden are) women already married except those who have fallen in your hand as prisoners of war"*

Surah 4:3 "And if you fear that you shall not be able to deal justly with the orphan-girls, then marry (other) women of your choice, two or three or four; but if you fear that you will not be able to deal justly (with them) then only one or (the slaves) that your right hands possess; That is nearer to prevent you from doing injustice."

Bukhari 7:20 "Narrated Abu Burda's father: Allah's Apostle said, any man who has a slave girl whom he educates properly, teaches good manners, manumits and marries her, will get a double reward. And if any man of the people of the Scriptures believes in his own prophet and then believes in me too, he will (also) get a double reward. And any slave who fulfills his duty to his master and to his Lord, will (also) get a double reward."

Thus, women captives were forced to marry their Muslim masters, regardless of the marital status of the women. That is, the masters are allowed to have sex with the enslaved women and they are considered their property, treated as non-humans, animals, toys. This however, is the norm for Islam and Muslims, women have absolutely "no human rights."

This sexual injustice is reprehensible, but Allah wills it nonetheless—the Koran verifies this. Predictably, the hadith also perpetuate this Koran-inspired immorality and human abuse, treating women with no rights, simply used as sex toys.

Thus, Muhammad believes that slave women who are part of the spoils of war can be treated like sexual property. Ali is a Muslim hero. He was the husband of Fatima, Muhammad's daughter by his first wife Khadija. Therefore Muhammad would not disallow his son-in-law the opportunity to have sex with a slave-girl. After all, slaves are fair sexual game, they are non-human, without rights; open targets for Muslim men.

Bukhari 7:137: Narrated Abu Said Al-Khudri: "We got female captives in the war booty and we used to do coitus interruptus with them. So we asked Allah's Apostle about it and he said, "Do you really do that?" Repeating the question thrice, "There is no soul that is destined to exist but will come into existence, till the Day of Resurrection."

Moreover, holy jihadists may not practice *coitus interruptus* with the women they capture, but not for the reason one expects: simple justice.

While on a military campaign and away from their wives, Muslim jihadists, received captives from among the Arab captives and said "we desired women and celibacy became hard on us and we loved to do *coitus interruptus.*" They asked Muhammad about this, and it is important to note what he did not say.

Muhammad did not scold them, condemn them or prohibit any kind of sex whatsoever, declaring it haram (forbidden). Rather, <u>he gets lost in ideology and the quirky doctrine of fate</u>:

"There is no soul that is destined to exist but will come into existence, till the Day of Resurrection."

Bukhari 5:459 Narrated Ibn Muhairiz: "I entered the Mosque and saw Abu Said Al-Khudri and sat beside him and asked him about Al-Azl (i.e. coitus interruptus). Abu Said said, "We went out with Allah's Apostle for the Ghazwa of Banu Al-Mustaliq and we received captives from among the Arab captives and we desired women and celibacy became hard on us and we loved to do coitus interruptus. So when we intended to do coitus interruptus, we said, 'How can we do coitus interruptus before asking Allah's Apostle who is present among us?' We asked (him) about it and he said, 'It is better for you not to do so, for if any soul (till the Day of Resurrection) is predestined to exist, it will exist."

That is, these inquiring Muslims should stop doing *coitus interruptus*, **but instead go all the way with the enslaved sex objects. Fate controls who should be born. Muhammad does not prohibit this extremely immoral practice.**

Simply stated, Islam legalizes rape.

The Koran does not abolish this sexual crime in the clearest terms: Thou shalt not have sex with slave-girls under any circumstance! The Koran authorizes just about every evil, wicked sexual act and deed without regard to human rights. Muhammad was a sex-crazed maniac; therefore he authorized every sexual appetite among Muslim men. The Koran upholds the practice.

Until religious Christian leaders renounce the Koran and the Hadith, for all its ungodly, unholy teachings, the world will be ravaged by the Islamic terrorism and trail of terror upon nation after nation. Women who are considering conversion to Islam "must stop" and think a second time, while they can still turn back.

Muhammad Marries Zainab

The following verse is about the story of Muhammad marrying Zainab, the wife of Muhammad's adopted son.

Surah 33:36 "it is not for a believer, man or woman, when Allah and his messenger have decreed a matter that they should have any option in their decision. And whoever disobeys Allah and his messenger, he has indeed strayed into a plain error."

But the capstone of these special marriages occurs when Muhammad also marries the ex- wife (Zaniab) of his adopted son (Zaid). His son–in–law divorces her with Muhammad lurking in the background. In fact, early Islamic sources say that Muhammad caught a glimpse of his daughter-in–law in a state of undress, and he desired her. Once the divorce is final, Allah reveals to him that this marriage between father-in-law and daughter–in–law is legal and moral in Surah 33:36-44. All of Muhammad's revelations were for his convenience, and were in fact, not revelations at all, but the perversions of a sick mind.

Surah 33:37 "And (remember) when you said to him (Zaid bin Harithah-the freed slave of the Prophet) on whom Allah bestowed grace (by guiding him to Islam) and you (O Muhammad) too have done favor (by manumitting him): Keep your wife to yourself and fear Allah. But you did hide in yourself (what was already made known to you that he will give her to you in marriage) that which Allah will make manifest, you did fear the people (i.e. their saying that Muhammad married the divorced wife of his released slave) whereas Allah had a better right that you should fear him..."

The Moral Problem With Such A Self–Serving Revelation

It was very clear that Muhammad was attracted to Zainab before Zaid divorced her and it might well have been the central reason for the divorce. The Koranic Surah itself makes it clear that there was something going on before Zaid's Divorce from Zainab. Muhammad simply declares, "It was Allah's will," and he just obeyed Allah. Who wants to question Allah's command?

There is more to this strange story. That this action is immoral and this revelation or justification of it is self-serving and not fitting according to the word of God is an important aspect. This is in contradiction to the true character of a "God", who demands moral purity, not compromise.

Surah 33:38-40 "There is no blame on the prophet in that which Allah has made legal for him. That has been Allah's way with those who have passed away of (the prophets of) old. And the command of Allah is a decree determined. Those who convey the message of Allah and fear him and fear none save Allah and sufficient is Allah as a reckoner. Muhammad is not the father of any of your men, but he is the messenger of Allah and the last (end) of the prophets. And Allah is ever All–aware of everything."

Bukhari 7:25 Narrated A'isha: "Abu Hudhaifa bin 'Utba bin Rabi'a bin Abdi Shams who had witnessed the battle of Badr along with the Prophet adopted Salim as his son, to whom he married his niece, Hind bint Al-Walid bin Utba bin Rabi'a; and Salim was the freed slave of an Ansar woman, just as the Prophet had adopted Zaid as his son."

Adoption of a Son

It was the custom that if somebody adopted a boy, the people would call him the son of the adoptive father and he would be the latter's heir. But when Allah revealed the Divine Surahs: 'Call them by (the names of) their fathers...your freed-slaves,' (33.5) the adopted persons were called by their fathers' names. The one's whose father was not known, would be regarded as a Maula and your brother in religion.

Bukhari 7:1 Narrated Anas bin Malik: "A group of three men came to the houses of the wives of the Prophet asking how the Prophet worshipped (Allah), and when they were informed about that, they considered their worship insufficient and said, "Where are we from the Prophet as his past and future sins have been forgiven." Then one of them said, "I will offer the prayer throughout the night forever." The other said, "I will fast throughout the year and will not break my fast." The third said, "I will keep away from the women and will not marry forever." Allah's Apostle came to them and said, "Are

you the same people who said so-and-so?
By Allah, I am more submissive to Allah
and more afraid of Him than you; yet I fast
and break my fast, I do sleep and I also
marry women. So, he who does not follow
my tradition in religion, is not from me (not
one of my followers)."

Bukhari 7:2 Narrated 'Ursa: that he asked 'Aisha
about the Statement of Allah: "If you fear
that you shall not be able to deal justly with
the orphan girls, then marry (other) women
of your choice, two or three or four; but if
you fear that you shall not be able to deal
justly (with them), then only one, or (the
captives) that your right hands possess. That
will be nearer to prevent you from doing
injustice.' (4.3) 'Aisha said, "O my nephew!
(This Verse has been revealed in connection
with) an orphan girl under the guardianship
of her guardian who is attracted by her
wealth and beauty and intends to marry her
with a Mahr less than what other women of
her standard deserve.   So they (such
guardians) have been forbidden to marry
them unless they do justice to them and give
them their full Mahr, and they are ordered to
marry other women instead of them."

Burkhari 7:6 Narrated Anas: "The Prophet used
to go round (have sexual relations with) all
his wives in one night, and he had nine
wives."

Bukhari 7:14 Narrated 'Aisha : I said, "O Allah's
Apostle! Suppose you landed in a valley

where there is a tree of which something has been eaten and then you found trees of which nothing has been eaten, of which tree would you let your camel graze?" He said, "(I will let my camel graze) of the one of which nothing has been eaten before." (The sub-narrator added: 'Aisha meant that Allah's Apostle had not married a virgin besides herself.)

Bukhari 7:15 Narrated A'isha: "Allah's Apostle said (to me), you have been shown to me twice in (my) dreams. A man was carrying you in a silken cloth and said to me, 'This is your wife.' I uncovered it; and behold, it was you. I said to myself, 'If this dream is from Allah, He will cause it to come true.' "

Bukhari 7:18 Narrated 'Ursa: "The Prophet asked Abu Bakr for A'isha's hand in marriage. Abu Bakr said "But I am your brother." The Prophet said, 'You are my brother in Allah's religion and His Book, but she (Aisha) is lawful for me to marry.' "

A Muslim man can marry as many as four women, and have sexual relations with an unspecified number of slaves as well. It is reported that Muhammad had thirteen wives and two concubines at one time. One of his wives was only six years old when Muhammad married her. Therefore, Muhammad should, with moral authority, be called a "demon-possessed pedophile."

Bukhari 1:268 " the prophet used to visit all wives in a round, during the day and night and they

were eleven in number, I asked Ana's had
the prophet the strength for it?" Ana's
replied we used to say that the prophet was
given the strength of thirty men."
Muhammad had special rules that allowed
him at least eleven wives (His successors
had more than four wives at a time as well.)

The Koran records that at one point Muhammad's
wives were so upset by Muhammad's taking a slave girl to
one of their own bedrooms that Allah once again had to step
down and whisper part of **Surah 33** in his ear, which
includes a threat to divorce them all if they didn't allow
Muhammad complete sexual freedom to do as he pleased.
The Koran is simply a collection of sayings of Muhammad
that gave him authorization to live as he pleased without
contradiction.

Surah 33:50 "O Prophet (Muhammad)! We have
made lawful to you your wives, to whom
you have paid mahr (bridal money given by
the husband to his wife at the time of
marriage), and those (slaves) whom your
right hand possesses-whom Allah has given
to you, and the daughters of your (paternal
and maternal uncles) and the daughters of
your (paternal and maternal aunts), who
have migrated (from Mecca) with you, and a
believing woman if she offers herself to the
Prophet, and if the Prophet wants to marry
her-a privilege for you only, not for the (rest
of) the believers..."

The text in **Surah 33:37** there is stated a particular purpose for this revelation and action of Muhammad. It is not for himself, but it is for the future of all Muslims. It is so that in the future there may not be a problem if anybody wants to marry the divorced wife of an adopted son. And this is the logical difficulty: Adoption is forbidden in Islam. This prohibition is based, for example, on these two texts from the same Surah.

Surah 33:4-5 "Allah has not made for any man two hearts inside his one body. Neither has he made your wives you declare to be like your mother's backs, your real mothers [the saying of the husband to the wife 'you are to me like the back of my mother,' (i.e. you are unlawful for me to approach)]: nor has he made your adopted sons your real sons. That is but your saying with your mouths. But Allah says the truth, and he guides to the right way. Call them (adopted sons) by the names of their fathers: that is more just with Allah. But if you know not their father's names, call them your brothers in faith, (and your freed slaves). And there is no sin on you concerning that which you made a mistake except in regard to what your hearts deliberately intend. And Allah is oft-forgiving, most merciful."

Without adoption, there cannot be any adopted son either. And so the explicitly stated reason for the revelation of this verse does not even exist. Muhammad himself dissolved the original adoption of Zaid when the above revelation came. Again, <u>the Koran is only the demonically delivered deception that dooms all of its followers</u>.

There are worse things in the world than polygamy (which has been practiced by other cultures outside of Islam), but it is shocking to see a religion place such value on a man's base cravings and sexual desire that he is permitted to bring other women into the marriage bed in order to satisfy his lust and passions. It causes women to be used as objects, toys, furniture, or any other property, rather than a human being that should have value, worth and human rights. The God of the Bible places a high value, real worth on women. There are no human rights in Islam.

Islam and its Koranic teachings devalue women and destroy their worth in society. When will America wake up and realize what is being pushed by the politically correct element in society is unholy and dangerous? We have leaders in Washington that are willing, even complicit in pushing for Sharia law which would allow this demonic Muslim teaching to become common in America. Every Christian must stand up, step up, and speak up while we still have an opportunity to do so. May God give us leaders that will protect our nation from the wiles of Islam.

"THE RECOMPENSE FOR THOSE WHO WAGE WAR AGAINST ALLAH AND HIS MESSENGER AND DO MISCHIEF IN THE LAND IS ONLY THAT THEY SHALL BE KILLED OR CRUCIFIED OR THEIR HANDS AND THEIR FEET BE CUT OFF FROM OPPOSITE SIDES, OR BE EXILED FROM THE LAND. THAT IS THEIR DISGRACE IN THIS WORLD, AND A GREAT TORMENT IS THEIRS IN THE HEREAFTER."

SURAH 5:33

17

Islam and HUMAN RIGHTS

Christians, Jews and all non-Muslims in Islamic countries are not safe. Although a non Muslim does not believe what the Koran says; they must follow the Koranic Sharia law in all aspects of life or face prosecution, jail, dismemberment or execution. There are no equal human rights, no freedom of expression, no different opinions allowed. Finding democracy where there are liberties and freedoms in Muslim countries is almost impossible. Muslim countries have long-lasting human tragedies such as, tyranny, corruption, ethnic-fighting, stoning, religious oppression, beheading, the cutting off of hands, feet, arms and legs, and the burning of Christian churches. Christians live in fear and silence every day. Muslim women are subjected to oppression, mutilation and humiliation. International terrorism finds support from all Islamic states. Most of the time, those who are oppressed by their governments themselves become oppressors when they obtain power or have opportunity. Authoritarian governments of Muslim countries such as Iran, Iraq, Libya,

Saudi Arabia, Turkey, Bangladesh, Pakistan, and Sudan are only a few examples of nations who institute crimes against humanity. They cannot be stopped without eliminating the sources of this terrorism. The reason for the lack of human rights is because of Koranic Law (Sharia); that is, a system of ideology dictated by the Koran and supported by the Hadith. The teachings of the Koran propel the followers of Allah to continue to oppress and murder. According to sociologists, it only takes 2% of any ethnic group to force issues and laws on the whole of a society. The U.S. has about twelve million Muslims.

Human Rights Violations in the Hadith

Bukhari 4:259 Narrated Abu Huraira: "Allah's Apostle sent us in a mission (i.e. An army-unit) and said, If you find so-and-so and so-and-so, burn both of them with fire. When we intended to depart, Allah's Apostle said, "I have ordered you to burn so-and-so and so-and-so, and it is none but Allah Who punishes with fire, so, if you find them, kill them."

Bukhari 4:260 Narrated Ikrima: "Ali burnt some people and this news reached Ibn 'Abbas, who said, "Had I been in his place I would not have burnt them, as the Prophet said, 'Don't punish (anybody) with Allah's Punishment.' No doubt, I would have killed them, for the Prophet said, 'If somebody (a Muslim) discards his religion, kill him.' "

Bukhari 4:261 Narrated Anas bin Malik: "A group of eight men from the tribe of 'Ukil came to the Prophet and then they found the climate of Medina unsuitable for them. So, they said, "O Allah's Apostle! Provide us with some milk. Allah's Apostle said, "I recommend that you should join the herd of camels." So they went and drank the urine and the milk of the camels (as a medicine) till they became healthy and fat. Then they killed the shepherd and drove away the camels, and they became unbelievers after they were Muslims. When the Prophet was informed by a shouter for help, he sent some men in their pursuit, and before the sun rose high, they were brought, and he had their hands and feet cut off. Then he ordered for nails which were heated and passed over their eyes, and they were left in the Harra (i.e. rocky land in Medina). They asked for water, and nobody provided them with water till they died. (Abu Qilaba, a sub-narrator said, "They committed murder and theft and fought against Allah and His Apostle, and spread evil in the land.")

Bukhari 4:265 Narrated Al-Bara bin Azib: "Allah's Apostle sent a group of the Ansar to Abu Rafi. Abdullah bin Atik entered his house at night and killed him while he was sleeping."

Bukhari 8:795 Narrated Anas: "The Prophet cut off the hands and feet of the men belonging to the tribe of 'Uraina and did not cauterize (their bleeding limbs) till they died."

Bukhari 1:234 Narrated Abu Qilaba: "Anas said Some people of 'Ukl or 'Uraina tribe came to Medina and its climate did not suit them. So the Prophet ordered them to go to the herd of (Milch) camels and to drink their milk and urine (as a medicine). So they went as directed and after they became healthy, they killed the shepherd of the Prophet and drove away all the camels. The news reached the Prophet early in the morning and he sent (men) in their pursuit and they were captured and brought at noon. He then ordered to cut their hands and feet (and it was done), and their eyes were branded with heated pieces of iron. They were put in 'Al-Harra' and when they asked for water no water was given to them." Abu Qilaba said, "Those people committed theft and murder, became infidels after embracing Islam and fought against Allah and His Apostle."

Bukhari 2:577 Narrated Ana's: "some people from 'Uraina tribe came to Medina and its climate did not suit them, so Allah's Apostle allowed them to go to the herd of camels (given as Zakat) and they drank their milk and urine (as medicine) but they killed the shepherd and drove away all the camels. So Allah's Apostle sent (men) in their pursuit to catch them, and they were brought, and he had their hands and feet cut, and their eyes were branded with heated pieces of iron and they were left in the Harra (a stony place at Medina) biting the stones.

No Justice or Human Rights in Islam

In Islam, there seems to be three main purposes of torture; to punish criminals, which include those who reject Islam, to extract information, and to exact revenge. But torture by its very nature is terror multiplied by terror, so it is wrong and unjust by its nature, thus it reveals no human rights found in Islamic law as fully dictated in the Koran.

Muhammad, the founder of Islam, asserts that his way is the best for all of humanity. He had this in mind when he tortured some captives who would not disclose where Jewish wealth lay hidden, and an old woman was taken as a prisoner in a Muslim raid. There is no sense of humanity in Islam; only revenge, terrorism and acts of Jihad against all who reject or disagree with Islam. Even when one drew a cartoon of Muhammad, all of Islam used that as a rationale to commit even further jihad resulting in more terror. A school teacher in California now lives under a death threat from Islam because she instructed her students to draw pictures of Muhammad.In order to justify this Islamic destruction of human rights, one of the oddest interpretive exercises performed by Muslim Scholars asserts that Jesus also endorsed torture and summary executions. Therefore, they assert, "who are Christians and the West (though the two are not identical) to complain about Islam?" The Lord Jesus Christ never endorsed such barbarism and murder. Where would Muslim apologists (defenders) find even a hint of it in the life and teachings of Christ? None, none whatsoever.

Jesus condemned murder; Muhammad commends torture, terror, jihad and terrorism against all non-Muslims.

Crucifixion and Mutilation in the Koran

Surah 5:33 "The recompense for those who wage war against Allah and His Messenger and do mischief in the land is only that they shall be killed or crucified or their hands and their feet be cut off from opposite sides, or be exiled from the land. That is their disgrace in this world, and a great torment is theirs in the hereafter."

In this Surah, Allah says that the criminal (according to Islam) who strives to spread corruption (any disagreement with Islam) in the land can be **(1)** executed, **(2)** crucified, **(3)** mutilated, or **(4)** expelled. There are problems in each form of punishment. Generally, there is no real trial or justice. Furthermore, there is no chance for the so-called criminal to redeem himself for the vague crime of corruption. There are no human rights in the Koran. It is one thing to execute a first-degree murderer, for example, but to torture a person by crucifixion, stoning or cutting off of the head is unacceptable for any country. Islam is authorization for this barbaric sense of justice and is perpetuated in the Koran. There are simply "no" human rights in all of Islamic tradition, teaching or text of the Koran or the Hadith. Muhammad practiced terrorism and his followers emulate him today around the world.

Splitting an Old Woman In Two

Perhaps the best way to explain and vivify this is to tell this story. Raiding of other cities or communities was part and parcel of seventh-century Arab culture, and Muhammad incorporated this demonic custom and elevated it to jihad. The raids (jihad terrorist attacks) were ugly, deadly and widespread. Muslims practice this in various forms today, that is, terrorism.

> "In early AD 628, during a raid, Zaid, Muhammad's freedman and adopted son, was wounded and some of his men were killed by a tribe. Zaid vowed to abstain from sex until he took revenge. After Zaid recovered from his wounds, Muhammad sent him and a raiding band back to the tribe. An old woman named Umm Qirfa was taken prisoner. Would a Muslim leader spare her from death, not to mention from torturing her? No. Her death was cruel, says an Islamic source, matter-of-factly. The executioner, appointed by Zaid, "tied each of her legs with a rope and tied the ropes to camels, and they split her in two." (Tabari)

It is not hard to imagine her anguish, horror and painful death. From the Islamic sources it is unclear why she, an old woman, had to die in the first place. Did an old woman have to die in such a gruesome way—by torture, which is grossly inhumane and hence always wrong? Islam sees nothing wrong with this. Some would argue that Muhammad himself did not order this torture, but that misses the point. The whole expedition was conducted under his orders. Muhammad did not even reprimand them, thus he approved the torture. Muhammad thought it right because of his demonic revelations called the Koran.

The following Hadith, although it does not mention the torture, recounts the aftermath of the raid. One of the raiders kept the daughter of Umm Qirfa for himself, and brought her back to Medina, where Muhammad lived. Upon seeing the girl, Muhammad shouted to the Muslim jihadist that he wanted her. What did he do with her? Sell her back to her family? Did he give her family the option to ransom her? Did he simply release her?

Muslim 8.4345 "Salama, a Muslim raider drove [captives] along until I brought them to Abu Bakr [Companion of Muhammad] who bestowed that girl on me as a prize. So we arrived in Medina. I had not yet disrobed her when the Messenger of Allah met me in the street and said: Give me that girl, O Salamah. I said: Messenger of Allah, she has fascinated me. I had not yet disrobed her. When on the next day, the Messenger of Allah again met me in the street, he said: O Salama, give me that girl, may God bless your father. I said: she is for you, Messenger of Allah. By Allah, I have not yet disrobed her. The Messenger of Allah sent her to the people of Mecca, and surrendered her as ransom for a number of

Muslims who had been kept as prisoners in Mecca."

Islam historically trafficked in slavery and allowed sex with women prisoners of war, in their most helpless, vulnerable condition. This Hadith gives a sad snapshot of slavery and human abuse in Islam. This still happens today in Islamic countries. Muhammad did not attempt to stop the raids, jihad or the violation of human rights. This activity generated a lot of money and fulfillment of sexual lust for Muslims. Again, another vivid illustration of the historic practice of no human rights in Islamic law.

Jihad Against Arabs

The following event provides the historical context of **Surah 5:33**. Shortly after Umm Qirfa's horrible death (perhaps only a few weeks or within the same month), some Arab tribesmen visited Muhammad and converted to Islam. But they fell sick in Medina. So Muhammad told them to follow a shepherd outside of the city, recommending to them an old folk belief for a cure: drinking the milk and urine of a camel. However, for some reason, they killed the shepherd, rejected Islam, and drove off the camels for themselves. This news reached Muhammad, and he ordered them to be hunted down and brought before him. He decreed that their hands and feet should be cut off. **Then he added these excesses on top of the others:**

Bukhari, Book of Jihad, no. 3018 "Then he ordered for [sic] nails which were heated

211

and [the tribesmen] were branded with those
nails, their eyes, and they were left in the
Harra (i.e. rocky land in Al-Medina). And
when they asked for water, no water was
given them till they died."

Human rights? Where are they in the history of Islam?
This is one of dozens of Surahs that validate the total lack of
human rights in Islam. Muhammad actually pierced their
eyes with nails (one version says with needles). Then, their
bodies were thrown on stony ground, dying of dehydration.
One version says they died from the battering they suffered
from being thrown on rocky ground; another says they died
from loss of blood, for Muhammad did not cauterize their
amputated limbs. This is none other than terrorism, jihad.

Abu Dawud, no. 4357 "When the Apostle of Allah
cut off (the hands and feet of) those who had
stolen his camels and he had their eyes put
out by fire (heated nails), Allah reprimanded
him on that (action), and Allah, the Exalted,
revealed: "The punishment of those who
wage war against Allah and His Apostle and
strive with might and main for mischief
through the land is execution or
crucifixion."

The problem with this Hadith is that it makes **Surah
5:33** appear as if it were a vast improvement of Muhammad's
ungodly actions. Though the text may improve on them a
little, the Koran still makes legal the torture and terrorism,
murder by crucifixion and mutilation. Both methods of
punishing criminals are excessive and therefore unjust

punishment, but it is validated in the Koran. In most of these cases, they had no hearing, no trial, no opportunity for redress; they were simply captured, terrorized and killed. No human rights.

The context of the following Surah in the Koran finds Muhammad confusedly relating the narrative about Moses confronting Pharaoh and his magicians. After seeing the power of God, the servants and magicians in Pharaoh's court believe in God, but the ruler will not stand for it. He threatens them with the same punishment that Allah and Muhammad authorize in **Surah 5:33**. <u>What a sham; an attempt to use the Bible for his acts of terrorism</u>, jihad upon jihad.

Surah 7:124 Says through the mouth of Pharaoh: "Surely, I will cut off your hands and your feet from opposite sides, then I will crucify you all."

Burning the Treasurer of the City of Khaybar

Muhammad conquered Khaybar in AD 628 (only a few months after the gruesome deaths of Umm Qirfa and the Arab tribesmen), but in AD 625, he had besieged and exiled the Jewish tribe of Nadir in Medina. They immigrated to Khaybar to the north. Muhammad wanted their treasure, not to mention the entire city, simply put, greed was at work. Ibn Ishaq the biographer writes about the torture of the treasurer, to extract information: Kinana b. al-Rabi, who had custody of the treasure of B. al-Nadir, was brought to Muhammad

213

who asked him about it. He denied that he knew where it was.

Muhammad and Found Treasure

"A Jew came to the apostle and said that he had seen Kinana going around a certain ruin every morning, early. When the apostle said to Kinana, "Do you know that if we find you have it, I shall kill you?" He said Yes. The apostle gave orders that the ruin was to be excavated and some of the treasure was found." **Pg. 515, "Life of Muhammad," Ibn Ishaq.**

Muhammad Permits Torture

"When he [Muhammad] asked him about the rest, he refused to produce it, so the apostle gave orders: "Torture him until you extract what he has," so [the torturer] kindled a fire with flint and steel on his chest until he was nearly dead." **Pg. 515, "Life of Muhammad," Ibn Ishaq.**

Throughout the history of Islam in any nation, or any part of the world you may seek but never find any evidence of "**Islamic**" human rights.

How does the story of the treasurer and Khaybar end? Kinana was beheaded in revenge for a killing, and Khaybar was conquered. The citizens, mostly Jews, could work the lands that now belonged to Islam by conquest, they had now to turn over half of their revenue and resources to

Muhammad and his special Muslim recipients. Islam always conquers, brings to subjection and submission through conversion, taxes or commission, if neither; then death. No human rights!

All Muslims and the Muslim nations following the teaching of Muhammad up to this day are doing the same things Muhammad did in seventh century, because that is the foundation, the belief and practices of Islam. None can find human rights offered or practiced in Islam.

"AND WHOEVER SEEKS A RELIGION OTHER THAN ISLAM, IT WILL NEVER BE ACCEPTED OF HIM AND IN THE HEREAFTER HE WILL BE ONE OF THE LOSERS."

SURAH 3:85

18

Islam and **LIBERTY**

The question may be asked, **"Is Islam compatible with the Christian's view of liberty?"** It is through this analysis that we will increase the understanding of Christians on this issue, thus better inform the world about Islamic teaching and the need to defend against Islamist Jihad, terrorism and global conquest. Unfortunately, multitudes of Christians are willfully ignorant of Islam and its deception regarding "liberty." By the question of Islam and liberty, we mean the relationship between ideas of freedoms like individual liberty, religious liberty, freedom of speech and tolerance, minority rights and the practice of Islam. Within Islamic teachings in the Koran and Islamic practice, **there are no human rights or liberty**. Yet, Dr. Parvez Ahmed, former National Director or C.A.I.R. was appointed to the Human Rights Commission in Jacksonville, Florida. "Human Rights Commission?" A World Net Daily Article dated 3/12/2010 addresses this issue as follows:

"Ohio authorities are investigating youth pastor Brian Williams for his assistance of

Rifqa Bary, 17, who claimed she fled her Muslim parents last year because her father threatened to kill her after learning she had become a Christian...I think this is another aspect of Islamic warfare that's going on, attempting to intimidate people into staying away from anything that may be considered a criticism of Islam. You can take action to save someone from harm. If you believe someone is in harm's way, you can take action to help...I am astonished the police and prosecutors have gone so far as to continue to go after Brian Williams...If you take seriously that apostates can be killed and have been killed, then it just doesn't make any sense that American law enforcement is investigating a youth minister who was acting basically to save a life...What kind of nation what kind of society are we living in where someone who helps a girl whose life is in danger is prosecuted for it? An Islamic one...A World Net Daily source said Bary now has been declared a dependent of the state of Ohio, a goal her defenders had adopted to protect the teen from any Muslim retribution for her decision to abandon Islam...Scholars in all the major streams of Islam have asserted the religion's holy book, the Koran, teaches that rejection of Islam must be punished by death."

On one hand the Koran asserts "let there be no compulsion in religion" and on the other hand there is no allowance to change from the Islamic faith.

Surah 2:256 "There is no compulsion in religion. Verily, the right path has become distinct from the wrong path. Whoever disbelieves in (all false deities) and believes in Allah, then he has grasped the most trustworthy handhold that will never break. And Allah is All-hearer All-knower..."

If anyone desires a religion other than Islam it never will be accepted; any Muslim who converts to another religion is considered an apostate and is to be killed.

Surah 3:85 "And whoever seeks a religion other than Islam, it will never be accepted of him and in the hereafter he will be one of the losers."

Islam has a history of violent treatment and death to those who leave it. The Koran speaks harshly of apostasy; an apostate will face the wrath of Allah in the hereafter. Women have no rights or liberty. Any Islamic woman that allows her face, arms or legs to be publicly displayed is subject to being stoned to death.

Surah 3:28 "Let not the believers take the disbelievers as (supporters or helpers) instead of the believers, and whoever does that will never be helped by Allah in any way except if you indeed fear a danger from them. And Allah warns you against himself (his punishment) and to Allah is the final return."

Surah 5:51 "O you who believe! Take not the Jews and Christians as (friends, protectors or helpers) they are but protectors of each other. And if any amongst you takes them, then surely he is one of them. Verily, Allah guides not those people who are the (polytheists and wrong doers)."

Surah 9:12 "But if they violate their oaths after their covenant and attack your religions with disapproval and criticism, then fight (you) the leaders of disbelief (chiefs of Quaraish pagans of Mecca)-for surely their oaths are nothing to them-so that they may stop (evil actions)."

Surah 9:14 "Fight against them so that Allah will punish them by your hands and disgrace them and give you victory over them and heal the breasts of a believing people."

Surah 9:123 "O you who believe! Fight those of the disbelievers who are close to you, and let them find harshness in you; and know that Allah is with those who are (the pious)."

Islamic law demands the punishment of death for apostasy from Islam, many traditions from the Islamic Hadith says **of those who changed their faith from Islam let them be killed.**

Because of this teaching and belief, Christians have been placed in great danger in missionary efforts towards Muslims and those who convert from Islam to Christianity face rejection persecution and death. **Thus, freedom of religion has not been an accepted liberty with Islam.** Most Muslim nations prohibit missionary activity, restrict or ban Bibles and churches, restricting the religious freedom of Christians, and place great roadblocks for building churches or growing of churches. In Africa, Pakistan, Saudi Arabia, Indonesia and all other Muslim nations or nations dominated by Islam, **Christianity is regulated, restricted or rejected totally.** There is no regard for religious or individual freedoms, liberty and **no tolerance for any change or question regarding the same**.

Let us pose a number of key questions that one may ask, perhaps, as benchmarks for people living in Muslim societies and states as to how they would relate to the issue of liberty and freedom.

How will Muslim states and societies treat religious minorities?

The key question to keep in mind is: Will they be treated as full and equal citizens, or will they be second-class citizens? The question about religious minorities is really one of equal rights before the law and equal citizenship. This question, for Islamic states and societies, is not so much a question of American experience. Yet, liberty will never be safe so long as it is assumed that the laws that govern men and women have, ultimately, an exclusively religious purpose. The Koran insists that "there shall be no coercion." However, this is only surface tolerance and attitude that is hardly the practice in Muslim societies; especially with the daily spread of Islamist ideologies and Koranic adherence in the world today. **Where Islam controls, liberty corrodes**

221

and freedoms are canceled. Christian churches in Pakistan, Indonesia, parts of Africa and other Islamic states or nations are being burned and Christians killed. Christian churches and Bibles are completely forbidden in Saudi Arabia. In Somalia (N. Africa) March 2011, sixty churches were burned and dozens of Christians murdered by invading Muslims.

> "Muslims are waging civil war against us, an undeclared "intifada" against the police with violent clashes injuring an average of 14 officers each day," according to Nicolas Sarkozy, Interior Minister of France.

How will Muslim societies and states deal with the rights of the individual?

It is difficult to understand how Muslims give the answer to this question (**usually it is a lie**) because there is not a difference between individual and group rights. Islam, as a religion, restricts or outright rejects both individual and group liberty. Once Islam has enough Muslims in a state or nation, they will demand "Sharia" law, that is, law according to the demonic book, "**The Koran**."

How will Muslim societies and states deal with freedom of expression and of the press?

In Islam, we can not find any respect for values that conform to a democracy and representative government. Until liberty as a principle in itself is seen in Muslim societies as a prerequisite for good governance and the practice of religion, we may question seriously that freedom of expression or the press will ever exist. Iran is a good example of NO freedom of press or liberty for its people. Saudi Arabia has "no" religious liberty for Christians; Bibles are banned and burned, Christian churches cannot be built and gospel tracts are forbidden. We only need to look at the chaos, confusion and jihad now taking place in the U.K., France, Germany, The Netherlands, London, and increasing in America. The uprising in Libya, Egypt and Yemen is nothing less than Holy War to bring about Sharia Law.

The final point is that non-Muslims cannot provide answers to these questions. The Muslims themselves must really give the answers and prove there is liberty in Islam. Most Muslim leaders will deny this in word, but their actions will affirm that there is no liberty; only the control of Islam. **In my study of the Koran, there is no liberty in Islam.** The Koran may state in a few places that religion is at liberty, however, a careful study of Islamic teachings in the Koran shows that **Islam recognizes "no" liberty or freedom for individuals or for Christianity.** In fact, all persons or organizations are forbidden to say anything considered negative about Muhammad or Islam. Anyone doing so is in danger of Islamic Jihad (Holy War) against them personally, as well as society in general. We all remember the events following the cartoon of Muhammad with a bomb in his bonnet. Muslims went on a frenzied jihad around the world. Also everyone recalls when Dr. Terry Jones of Gainesville, FL, announced his intentions to burn the Koran. Every

Muslim went into jihad mode. Where is the freedom? Where is the liberty?

We must keep in mind that in Christ we are free, and **in Islam, a person is enslaved to a demonic book (the Koran) and their prophet, Muhammad, a demon-possessed pedophile.**

While the U.S. and global media had a field day in Florida, and on every network, over the announcement of the planned Koran burning, the nation did not hear of the case of Bibles burned in Afghanistan. An American soldier received a case of Bibles printed in Arabic, paid for and shipped by his church in the U.S. The young soldier, risking his life on Muslim soil, simply was attempting to witness for Jesus. He had Bible studies in his barracks. When this was discovered, his station commander ordered the chaplain to take the Bibles. They confiscated the Bibles and **"burned them."** They said they did not want to offend the Muslims. **Freedom, liberty in Islam? Where?**

19

$\mathscr{I}\!\mathit{slam}$ and TOLERANCE

Webster's New International Dictionary defines tolerance as: "to endure, put up with," "a permissive or liberal attitude towards beliefs or practices differing from or conflicting with one's own," "sympathy or indulgence for diversity in thought or conduct."

America, as well as most of the Western World, have practiced "tolerance" toward Islam, thus, there are over 3,000 mosques already on U.S. soil, and hundreds more in every stage of planning and building. Islam, however, never has been tolerant because the demonic book, the Koran, forbids any tolerance for a non-Muslim.

Surah 27:59 Say (O Muhammad)! Praise and thanks be to Allah, and peace be on his slaves whom he has chosen (for his message)..."

However, the true gauge of peace is not found in one's conduct toward only those of the same faith or religion, but rather in the behavior shown to others.

Though peace is charged and even claimed, it is easily displaced by **intolerance, hatred** and **warring**; the killing (Jihad) that is carried out by Islamics everywhere. The Koran instructs,

Surah 9:29 **"Fight those who believe not in Allah nor the Last Day,** nor forbid that which has been forbidden by Allah and His Messenger, and those who acknowledge not the religion of truth (i.e. Islam), among the people of the Scripture (Jews and Christians), **until they pay the Jizyah (tribute) with submission and feel themselves subdued."**

Surah 8:65 "O Prophet (Muhammad)! **Urge the believers to fight.** If there are twenty steadfast persons amongst you, you will overcome two hundreds, and if there are a hundred steadfast persons they will overcome a thousand of those who disbelieve, because they (the disbelievers) are people who do not understand."

A command which is given (i.e., to be peaceful to 'unbelievers'), may be supplanted (abrogated) [See Chapter 3] by a subsequent directive (i.e., to kill 'unbelievers'). Indeed, the frequency of commands to deal peacefully and with forbearance fails in comparison to those which encourage and command fighting, killing and destruction upon unbelievers (non-Muslims).

The Obligation of Jihad to Tolerate Others

Much attention has been given to the word "Jihad" by Islamic scholars, Christian leaders, and many other interested parties. In the following Surah, "Jihad" can be considered an inner struggle for purity. However, **Jihad is far beyond just an inner struggle, it is the only sure way for Muslims to get to paradise.**

Surah 29:69 "As for those who strive hard in Us (our cause), We will surely guide them to Our paths(i.e. Allah's religion-Islamic monotheism). And verily Allah is with the good doers."

Jihad can also refer to an intellectual struggle

Surah 25:52"...Obey not the disbelievers, but strive against them (by preaching) with the utmost endeavor with it (the Koran)."

Physical Warfare-Jihad

However, the most prominent use of *"Jihad"* is in reference to physical warfare. Allah insists:

Surah 61:9-11 "He it is who sent His Messenger (Muhammad) with guidance and the Religion of Truth, to make **it victorious over all other religions, even though the unbelievers (non-Muslims) hate it.** O you who believe! Shall I guide you to a trade that will save you from a painful torment? That you believe in Allah and His Messenger and strive hard and fight in the cause of Allah with your wealth and your lives: that will be better for you, if you but know!"

The Koran Declares

Surah 2:190, 193 "And fight in the way of Allah those who fight you, but transgress not the limits. Truly, Allah likes not the transgressors... **And fight against them until there is no more disbelief, and the religion is for Allah**. But if they cease, let there shall be no transgression except against the harm doers (all non-Muslims)."

The Muslim is not to be an aggressor, but is justified and commanded to use force against the enemy (non-Muslims). Any system, religion or nation that will not allow Islam to control is seen as the enemy, thus the aggressor. This is seen in terrorist plotting, planning, training, and preparation for the ultimate jihad against America. America has over 40 Islamic jihad planning, training centers, all known by Homeland Security and the F.B.I., yet nothing is being done to prevent the activation.

The Koran and Tolerance

It is commendable when one, believing to have the truth, makes a considerable effort to share it with others. However, Islam not only commands the Muslim to take the religion of Allah forth, but to overcome and terrorize those who oppose by force. **Followers of Islam have a mandate to fight until Islam is the only religion.** Islam believes that they are to dominate the world during the 21st

228

century.Tolerance towards any non-Muslim is tantamount to sin according to the Koran. The conversion of the entire global population to Islam and the complete extinction of every other form of religion is the goal of the Islamic world.

Surah 3:19: "truly the religion of Allah is Islam...whoever disbelieves, Allah will judge."

Surah 3:85: "Whoever seeks a religion other than Islam, it will never be accepted..."

Surah 4:56: "Those who disbelieve...we shall burn them in fire..."

If any infidel is allowed to exist in the community, state or nation, it is only a necessary evil, and for only a transitional period. Political, social, and financial burdens or disabilities must be imposed on him to ultimately cause him to submit to Islam.

Surah 2:6-7 "Verily, those who disbelieve, (non-Muslims) it is the same to them whether you warn them or do not warn them, they will not believe. **Allah has set a seal on their hearts, and on their hearing, and on their eyes there is a covering. Theirs will be a great torment.**"

Surah 2:286, 3:147 "...**Give us victory over the disbelieving (non-Muslims) people.**"

Surah 3:28 "**Let not the believers take disbelievers (non-Muslims) for their friends** in preference to believers (Muslims)."

Surah 3:32 "...Allah does not like the disbelievers (non-Muslims)."

Surah 3:56 "As to those who disbelieve (non-Muslims) I will punish them with a severe torment in this world and in the Hereafter; and they will have no helpers."

Surah 3:85 "Whosoever seeks as religion other than Islam, it will never be accepted of him, and in the Hereafter he will be one of the losers."

Surah 4:91 "...Take (hold of) them and kill them wherever you find them. In their case We have given you clear warrant against them."

Surah 4:101 "Verily, the disbelievers (non-Muslims) are ever an open enemy to you."

Surah 4:144 "O you who believe! Take not disbelievers (non-Muslims) for (your) friends instead of believers (Muslims). Do you offer Allah a manifest proof against yourselves?"

Surah 5:51 "O you who believe! Take not the Jews and the Christians as friends...And if any amongst you who takes them (as friends), then surely he is one of them."

Surah 8:38-39 "Say to those who have disbelieved, if they cease (from disbelief) their past will be forgiven. But if they return (thereto), then the examples of those (punished) before them have already preceded (as a warning). And **Fight them until there is no more**

disbelief and the Religion will be for Allah alone (in the whole world)."

Surah 9:73 "**O Prophet (Muhammad)! Strive hard against the disbelievers (non-Muslims) and the hypocrites, and be harsh against them,** their abode is hell, and worst indeed is that destination."

Surah 9:113 "It is not proper for the Prophet, and those who believe, to ask forgiveness of idolaters (non-Muslims), even though they may be of kin, after it has become clear to them that they are dwellers of the Fire."

Surah 9:123 "O you who believe! **Fight those of the disbelievers** (non-Muslims) who are close to you, and let them find harshness in you; and know that Allah is with the pious."

Surah 22:15 "Whoever thinks that Allah will not help him (Muhammad) in this world and the Hereafter, let him stretch out a rope to the ceiling and let him strangle himself. Then let him see whether his plan will remove that whereat he rages!"

Surah 58:22 "You (O Muhammad) will not find any people who believe in Allah and the Last Day, making friendship with those who oppose Allah and His messenger, even though they were their fathers or their sons or their brothers or their kindred (people)..."

Surah 60:1 "O you who believe! Take not My enemies and your enemies as friends showing affection towards them while they have disbelieved in what has come to you of the truth…"

Surah 60:13 "O you who believe! Take not as friends the people who incurred the wrath of Allah (the Jews). Surely they have despaired of (receiving any good in) the Hereafter…"

Surah 66:9 "O Prophet (Muhammad)! Strive hard against the disbelievers (non-Muslims) and the hypocrites, and be severe against them, their abode will be Hell and worst indeed is that destination."

Surah 5:33 "The recompense of those who wage war against Allah and His Messenger and do mischief in the land is only that **they shall be killed or crucified, or their hands and their feet be cut off from opposite sides,** or be exiled from the land. That is their disgrace in this world, and a great torment in the Hereafter."

Time and again, the Koran commands "Fight in the way of Allah." Regardless of whether a Muslim ever openly admits it or not, his heart, his goal, aim and intent is to destroy all non-Muslims.

The Example of Muhammad

The Koran entreats Muslims to worship Allah, and Him alone. Muhammad is to all Muslims an example to follow after in the service of Allah. Muhammad is the ultimate example in Islam.

Surah 48:29 "Muhammad is the Messenger of Allah, And those who are with him are severe against disbelievers but are merciful among themselves..."

Bukhari 1:24 "narrated by Aisha the prophet said "I declared of himself: I have been ordered to fight against the people until they testify that none has the right to be worshipped but Allah and that Muhammad is Allah's Apostle, and offer the prayers perfectly and give the obligatory charity..."

So, it is that **a study of Muhammad's life in the Koran reveals him to be a man of war.** He was a man of the sword, and incited those who would follow him to be likewise. Today, those who are Muslims will themselves be as Muhammad was. They will declare religion to be of Allah, and **fight and destroy through Jihad all who stand in opposition.** Jihad in its many forms is being practiced in America today. The planned Cordoba Mosque at ground zero is a form of Jihad, emotional warfare.

When we consider carefully the nature of Islam, though it speaks of peace, tolerance and equality, the **Koran's self proclaimed right of abrogation (see Chapter 3) reduces these claims to empty words**. The overall picture of the Koran is one of violence and intolerance to non-Muslims. The directives and comments of all Islamic leaders motivate followers to war against non-Muslims. Muhammad, the prophet of Allah, was himself a violent man, killing those who opposed his religion. **Without a doubt, Islam teaches**

its followers to be violent, intolerant, and has an agenda to globalize for Allah and Islam.

World Net Daily carried a news article dated July 22, 2010, of two Christian pastors who were killed by a mob of rioting Muslims. These two pastors were shot and killed on their way to a courthouse from jail after being accused by Pakistani Muslims of "blaspheming Muhammad." The two pastors had not been convicted, just accused. The killing of "a blasphemer" is the clearest example of Sharia law (law according to the Koran). It is a perfect example of Muhammad. The word or deed called tolerance is simply not compatible with Muslims or Islam in any sense of the word.

Imam Abdul Rauf fully expressed his intolerance in an interview on national television regarding the ground zero mosque, when he threatened America with (terrorists) Jihad if the planned mosque is not built near the ruins of 9/11 where almost 3,000 died at the hands of Islamic terrorists in a Jihad against America.

Islamic Law and Tolerance

According to Robert Spencer as stated in his book, **"The Myth of Islamic Tolerance**," page 63, we find the legal ordinances which are enforced on all Christians and Jews who reside in Muslim countries.

1. Christians and Jews are not allowed to build churches, temples or synagogues.

2. Christians and Jews are not allowed to pray or read their sacred books out loud at home or in churches, lest Muslims hear their prayers.

3. Christians and Jews are not allowed to print their religious books or sell them in public places.

4. Christians and Jews are not allowed to install crosses or Stars of David on their houses or churches, since they are a symbol of infidelity.

5. Christians and Jews are not allowed to broadcast or display their services on radio, television or other media.

6. Christians and Jews are not allowed to congregate publically.

7. Christians and Jews cannot join the army because they are not allowed to assume leadership positions.

Islam is therefore the most intolerant religion in the world. Yet, the Christian is accused of not being tolerant.

The Koran literally precludes any tolerance:

Surah 6:34: "…And none can alter the words (decisions)of Allah…"

Surah 10:64: "…No change can there be in the words of Allah…"

Any Muslim that believes, reads or follows the words of the Koran cannot tolerate the words, deeds, teachings, doctrines or theology of the Christian or the Western World.

"THINK NOT OF THOSE WHO ARE KILLED IN THE WAY OF ALLAH AS DEAD. NAY THEY ARE ALIVE WITH THEIR LORD AND THEY HAVE PROVISION."

SURAH 3:169

20

Islam and **MARTYRDOM**

The Koran declares that a Muslim that is killed in Allah's way is not dead but alive. This simply interpreted to mean that any Muslim who is killed in a Jihad attains automatic salvation and is immediately in paradise. Though some Muslims deny this and deny holy war, yet it is very clear in the teachings of the Koran. The attackers of 9-11 who thought they would go directly to paradise are now burning in Hell for their actions. Perhaps they are wondering when the jet fuel will stop burning, but it is the flames of Hell.

Surah 3:157-158 "And if you are killed or die in the way of Allah, forgiveness and mercy from Allah are far better than all that they amass (of worldly wealths): and whether you die or are killed verily unto Allah that you shall be gathered."

Surah 22:58-59 "those who emigrated in the cause of Allah, (Jihad) and after that were killed or died, surely Allah will provide a good provision for them... Truly he will make

them enter an entrance with which they shall
be well pleased..."

Surah 3:169 "Think not of those who are killed in
the way of Allah as dead. Nay they are alive
with their lord and they have provision."

While much of the Islamic ideology of Jihad predates
the religion of Islam, Islam was born in a harsh, demanding
environment where fighting, murder and death were
common. The ideology of martyrdom and suffering as
encapsulated in the Koran is accepted and followed by
Muslims around the world. The distinct themes in the Koran
and Hadith proved a powerful and volatile combination: **the
call to war, the call to martyrdom and the martyr's
rewards.** This is one of the key requirements of Islam for all
able bodied Muslims. The passages in the Koran explain that
martyrdom in the cause of Allah is a means to enter paradise.
In fact, martyrdom (in jihad) is the only guarantee of
paradise.

Bukhari 2:329 "Allah's Apostle said someone
came to from my Lord and gave me the
news that if any of my followers dies
worshipping none along with Allah he will
enter."

Abu dawud 14:2535 says "the Apostle of Allah if
anyone fights in Allah's path and die the
paradise will be assured from him. If
anyone sincerely asks Allah for being Killed
and dies or is killed there will be a reward of
a martyr from him if anyone suffers from

ulcers will in Allah's path, he will have on
him the stamp of the martyrs."

Such passages as these provide much of the rationale
for a further ideological position: not only does a martyr in
the cases of Allah enter paradise, **but he does so
automatically—his admission is guaranteed**. Further
rewards, as reported by the Hadith are that the fighter in
Allah's cause will, if killed in the struggle, receive otherwise
unattainable (he escapes the examination in the grave by the
interrogating Angels): he does not need to pass through
(barzakh) the purgatory limbo, he receives the highest of
ranks in paradise, sitting near the throne of Allah.
Muhammad described the "house of martyrs" (dar- al
shuada) as the most beautiful abode of paradise. **He, as a
martyr, will be given 72 black eyed virgins for eternity**.
What will Muslim women jihadists receive in paradise?
Many Hadith elaborate on this theme, such as this in Sahih
Bukhara:

Bukhari, Book of Jihad, No. 2606: Narrated
Samurai: "The prophet said last night two
men came to me in dream and made me
ascend a tree and then admitted me into a
better and more superior house, better of
which I have never seen one of then said this
house is the house of martyrs."

On the Day of Judgment, any wounds the martyr
received in battle will shine and smell like musk: his death as
a martyr frees him of all such sin. Such that he does not
require the intercession of the prophet; he is purified by his

act of Jihad and so he alone is not washed before burial. The pictorial understanding of the Koran depicts of this paradise for the believer (Muslim) (martyr or not) could only be the highest goal and the greatest appeal to every Muslim; awaiting him is a garden of cool breezes, beautiful companions (72 virgins), couches, fruit and drink, and nearness to Allah. Particularly deserving martyrs (those who kill many in jihad) are even eligible for double the standard reward. This was the incentive of the 9-11 Islamic terrorists that murdered almost three thousand people. This incentive is so great that Muhammad is reported to have said that no one who dies and enters paradise; would wish to come back to this world, even if he were to be given ownership of the whole world and whatever is in it, except the martyr who, on seeing the superiority of martyrdom, would like to come back to the world and get killed again." What a lie from Satan and all of his demons! Only Hell awaits the one who commits murder in the name of Allah.

Bukhari 4:53 Narrated Ana's bin Malik, "The prophet said nobody who dies and finds Good from Allah in the hereafter would wish to come back to this world even if he were given the whole word and whatever is in it, except the martyr who on seeing the superiority of martyrdom would like to come back to the world and get killed again in Allah's cause."

This is the aspect of martyrdom which best helps interpret an apparent contradiction. The modern Muslim form of jihad often features, and is notorious for, a new willingness to embrace suicide in the prosecution of the battle and a new fervor in seeking martyrdom. Yet in another Surah, the Koran expressly forbids suicide:

Surah 2:195 "...do not throw yourselves into your own destruction..."

Bukhari 2:446 narrated Abu Huraira "the prophet said he who commits suicide by throttling shall keep on throttling himself in the hell of fire forever and he who commits suicide by stabbing himself shall keep on stabbing himself in the hell of fire."

According to these preceding Surahs of the Koran and the text of the Hadith teach that anyone who dies by suicide will eternally reenact said suicide in hell. These Surahs have been abrogated (see Chapter 3), thus the Surahs teaching death by jihad are followed and obeyed.

In the other Surahs we have seen allows us to clarify now the reasons why martyrdom, even more than the aspect referred to as spiritual striving, **jihad is the most uniquely religious aspect of Islam**, and <u>desired of every believing Muslim without exception</u>. It's not just a radical, small portion of Islam, but every Muslim who believes the Koran. There is no moderate or radical Islam, just "Islam."

Muhammad limited the proper sphere of war solely to fighting in the path of Allah: purely political conflicts, yet today any social, economic or political struggle is in view. In Muhammad's philosophy, any war he sanctioned has, more than just political, it also had another dimension. These wars had spiritual justification, and thus, anyone killed while fighting in one of them was not merely a dead soldier but was a warrior, witness, martyr of Allah.

Another dimension which makes death in Jihad wholly unlike death in a secular conflict is that the soldier in a political war would seek to defeat his adversary while preserving his own life. A death thereby incurred would be no more than an unfortunate accident. **The soldier who dies in the path of Allah, however, accepts and embraces his death, for the religious back drop to the jihad guarantees his fate**; assures him a place in paradise. A Muslim can practice the five pillars of Islam and never be assured Paradise, but the Muslim that dies in holy war, jihad, is guaranteed Paradise.

The martyr in Islam is guaranteed a unique reward–automatic admittance to Paradise. Of the host of specific honors promised the martyr is none other than religious, which implies that religion, (not secular factors like political gain or strategic advantage) is the chief justification for participating in a Jihad. **All the five pillars of Islam can not guarantee paradise, but Jihad does.**

21

Islam and **JIHAD**

Muhammad taught his followers to oppress, terrorize or kill all non-Muslims. Generally, Jews and Christians were allowed to live, provided they paid (Jizyah), a special tax which was an indicator of their submission to Islam. This jizyah, tax was revenue given to the Muslims for what could only be seen as "protection money," that is, having to pay the Islamic leaders to prevent them from killing you. If the Jews and Christians refused to pay this extortion tax, they were to convert to Islam or be killed. Even non-Jews and non-Christians, such as idolaters or pagans, had to convert to Islam or be killed. Generally, they didn't have the option of paying the jizyah tax. **Here are the Surahs that teach Muslims to kill or oppress Jews and Christians wherever they kind them.**

Surah 9:29 "Fight against those who believe not in Allah nor in the Last Day, nor forbid that which has been forbidden by Allah and his messenger (Muhammad), and those who acknowledge not the religion of truth, (which is Islam that abolishes all other religions) among the people of the Scripture." (Jews and Christians) until they pay the jizyah (the tax imposed upon them) with willing submission and feel themselves subdued."

Surah 4:89 "...But if they turn back (from Islam) take (hold of) them and kill them wherever you find them..."

Surah 47:4 "So, when you meet (in fight— Jihad in Allah's Cause), those who disbelieve, smite (their) necks till when you have killed and wounded many of them, then bind a bond firmly (on them, i.e. take them as captives). Thereafter (is the time) either for generosity (i.e. free them without ransom), or ransom (according to what benefits Islam), until the war lays down its burden. Thus [you are ordered by Allah to continue in carrying out Jihad against the disbelievers (non-Muslims) till they embrace Islam (i.e. are saved from the punishment in the Hell-fire) or at least come under your protection], but if it had been Allah's Will, He Himself could certainly have punished them (without you). But (He lets you fight), in order to test some of you, with others. But those who are killed in the Way of Allah, He will never let their deeds be lost."

Surah 9:123 "O you who believe! Fight those of the disbelievers who are close to you, and let them find harshness in you, and know that Allah is with those who are the pious."

Surah 8:67 "It is not for a Prophet that he should have prisoners of war (and free them with ransom) until he had made a great slaughter (among his enemies) in the land. You desire the good of this world (i.e. the money of ransom for freeing the captives), but Allah desires (for you) the Hereafter. And Allah is All-Mighty, All-Wise."

Surah 8:59-60 "And let not those who disbelieve think that they can outstrip (escape from the punishment). Verily, they will never be able to save themselves (from Allah's Punishment). And make ready against them all you can of power, including steeds of war (tanks, planes, missiles, artillery, etc.) to threaten the enemy of Allah and your enemy, and others besides whom, you may not know but whom Allah does know. And whatever you shall spend in the Cause of Allah shall be repaid unto you, and you shall not be treated unjustly."

Surah 8:36 "Verily, those who disbelieve spend their wealth to hinder (men) from the Path of Allah, and so will they continue to spend it; but in the end it will become an anguish for them. Then they will be overcome. And those who disbelieve will be gathered unto Hell."

The instruction to subjugate or kill Christians and Jews is in the Koran. It is clear that Muhammad ordered his followers to fight Christians and Jews so as to convert them or pay the jizyah tax. However, if they didn't convert to

Islam or pay the tax they would be killed: Do you think that he told the followers to let them go in peace? Islam has never taught or allowed anything other than convert to Islam or be killed. It is very clear convert; pay with submission, or die. The background for this is found in the book: "**The Life of Muhammad**" by Ibn Ishaq:

> "Until they the Jews and Christians pay the poll tax out of hand being humbled as a compensation for what you fear to lose by the closing of the markets, Allah gave you compensation for what he removed from you in your former polytheism by what he gives you by way of poll tax leveled on the people of scripture."

Muhammad told his followers to attack the Jews and Christians. If they humbled themselves and submitted to the Muslims and chose to remain Christian or Jewish, then they had to pay the jizyah tax to the Muslims. This is simply a way of causing a non-Muslim to submit and be in subjection of Islamic Law (Sharia rule). Again, as Muhammad's circumstances changed, Allah (according to Muhammad) changed and gave new revelations. Also note that the tax levied upon the Christians and Jews was not to support the state in general affairs; it was to compensate the Muslims. Muhammad was exactly like a mafia crime boss; extorting money for the protection from the Muslims. We find the following Surah in the Koran that teaches Muslims to **attack and kill the non-Muslims**:

Surah 9:5 "Then when the sacred months (the 1st, 7th, 11th and 12th months of the Islamic calendar) have passed, then kill the idolaters wherever you find them, and capture and besiege them, and lie in wait for them in each and every ambush. But if they repent and pray and give zakat, then leave their way clear. Allah is oft-forgiving, most merciful."

Again, the background for this Surah is found in "**The Life of Muhammad**." Comments to clarify the sense of the quotation are placed within brackets. **The entire passage is a very long one, so only a brief portion of it is quoted:**

"A discharge came down, Muhammad received a supposed revelation from Allah permitting the breaking of the agreement between the apostle and the polytheists; (Muhammad viewed Christians as polytheists because of the belief in the Trinity) meanwhile, there were particular agreements between the apostle and the Arab tribes for specified terms. And there came down about it and about the disaffected that held back from him in the raid on Tabuk, a Christian town Muhammad attacked, and a proclamation from them to pay him. So travel through the land for four months and know that you cannot escape Allah and that Allah will put the unbelievers to shame. And a proclamation from Allah and his apostle (Muhammad) to men on the day of the greater pilgrimage, that Allah and his apostle are free from obligation to polytheists, (i.e., after this pilgrimage). So, if you repent, it will be better for you; and if you turn back, know that you cannot escape Allah. **Inform these who disbelieve (in Islam), about a painful punishment except those polytheists with whom you have made a treaty**, if one of the polytheists (i.e. one of these whom I have ordered you to kill), asks your protection, give it him so that he may have protection; convey him to his place of safety."

Basically stated, Muhammad had an agreement with a number of Arab tribes. Some were peaceful with him. Others disliked him. Allah supposedly gives Muhammad a revelation allowing him to break his word (the agreement with the pagan [non-Muslims and the Arabs]) and attack them until the four sacred months were over. Once again, Muhammad had gained power and things changed, he received new so-called revelations from Allah. **Muhammad was then permitted to lie (i.e., break his agreement and make war against the pagans {non-Muslims}).** Muhammad's circumstances changed, and Allah served Muhammad as a means to authorize his changing. Note that in the last quoted paragraph, Allah is telling the Muslims to go out and kill people. Some of these people had gotten along peacefully with the Muslims, but because they didn't follow Muhammad, they were to be attacked, subdued and killed if they refuse to convert to Islam.

"Islamization of a nation begins where there are sufficient Muslims in a country to agitate (push, demand) for their religious rights."

Free Republic, 2/5/2010

Islam's official position can be stated in this way; **"while small, comply, when strong, conquer."**

Islamic Killing of All Who Leave Islam

Muhammad was not content to conquer by force or kill these who merely opposed him verbally. Muhammad also taught that Muslims who leave the Islamic faith are to be murdered as well. Here are some quotes from Bukhari's collection of Hadith. **Remember, Bukhari Hadith is the second-most important writing in Islam following the Koran.**

Bukhari 9:17 Narrated Abdullah: Allah's Apostle said, "The blood of a Muslim who confesses that none has the right to be worshipped but Allah and that I am his Apostle, cannot be shed except in three cases: in qisas (equality in punishment) for murder, a married person who commits illegal sexual intercourse and the one who reverts from Islam (apostate) and leaves the Muslims."

Bukhari 9:57 Narrated Ikrima, "Some atheists were brought to Ali and he burnt them. The news of this event reached Ibn Abbas who said, if I had been in his place, I would not have burnt them, as Allah's apostle forbade it saying, do not punish anybody with Allah's punishment (fire). I would have killed them according to the statement of Allah's apostle. Whoever changed his Islamic religion then kill him."

Bukhari 9:64 Narrated Ali "whenever I tell you a narration from Allah's apostle, by Allah I would rather fall down from the sky, than ascribe a false statement to him, but if I tell you something between me and you, not a Hadith, then it was indeed a trick (i.e. I may say things just to cheat my enemy). No doubt I heard Allah's apostle saying during the last days there will appear some young foolish people who will say the best words but their faith will not go beyond their throats, (i.e. they will have no faith) and will go out from (leave) their religion as an arrow goes out of the game. So wherever you find them kill them, for whoever kills them shall have reward on the day of resurrection."

Muhammad intimidated, subdued, dismembered and murdered people to propagate his ideology, all as a holy war (jihad). **His actions were the actions of ideological, political and religious terrorism.** It is the same ideology and terrorism practiced in the world today. Since Muslims look to Muhammad as a source of inspiration and a model of behavior, **Muslims find support for Islamic terroristic activity in the life and teachings of their prophet Muhammad.** Today, Muslims use the Koran as a justification to attack and murder those who reject Muhammad or the demonic book called the Koran and Islam.

When Muslim terrorists do this, they are following faithfully in Muhammad's footsteps according to the teachings of the Koran and Hadith. Jesus condemned those who murder and Muhammad falls into this category, therefore we conclude that **Muhammad is not a saint, he was a lost, terrorist murderer who, according to the Bible, is in Hell.** Remember Muhammad commends murder, but Jesus condemns murder. We find jihad as a command directed to all Muslims enforced by the Koran. The focus of Jihad is to overcome and destroy people who do not accept Islam. Christians and Jews were persecuted and killed on a regular basis, as well as people who were idol worshipers, anyone who did not convert to Islam.

> "We are in a state of civil war orchestrated by Islamists. This is not a question of urban violence any more, it is an 'intifada:" We need armored vehicles and water cannons. They are the only things that will disperse crowds of hundreds of people (Muslims) trying to kill us."
>
> Nicolas Sarkozy
> Interior Minister, France

Surah 2:217 "They ask you concerning fighting in the sacred months (i.e. 1st 7th 11th and 12th months of the Islamic calendar). Say 'fighting therein is a great (transgression), but a greater (transgression) with Allah is to prevent mankind from following the way of Allah, to disbelieve in him, to prevent access to Al-masjid –Al-haram (at Mecca) and to drive out its inhabitants, and Al-Fitnah is worse than killing.' They will never cease fighting you until they turn you back from your religion if they can. And whosoever of you turns back from his religion and dies as a disbeliever, then his deeds will be lost in this life and the hereafter, and they will be the dwellers of the fire. They will abide therein forever."

According to the UK Times Online newspaper, Sheikh El Faisal instructed his followers on ways to murder non-Muslims, as a "wonderful" act that would ensure them (Muslims) immediate entry into paradise, (1-23-2003).

Do we have terrorist, jihadists in America? The answer is emphatically "yes." The F.B.I., C.I.A., and Homeland Security all know the depth and breadth of the jihadist training camps in America. David Hurd of CBN News, August 4, 2006, provided a map of the terrorist network in America. See map on next page for details.

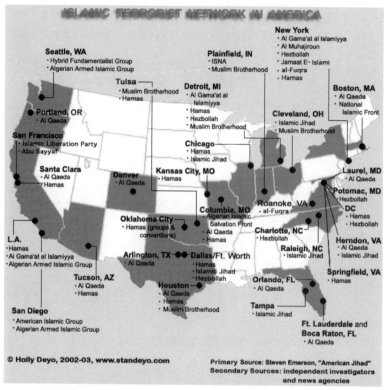

NOTE: Terrorists are a very real and growing threat in America and to American interests around the world. It should be *assumed* these are not the only cell locations within the US and that they are subject to change. For more information, see Prudent Places USA on the world wide web.

The Different Kinds of Jihad

According to Dr. Robert Morey, in his book, "**An Analysis of the Hadith**," page 16-17, lists five different jihads:

1. **Jihad of Taxation**: For those who refuse to accept Islam, but live under Islamic rule.

2. **A Jihad of Reward**: A free university education for any Christian or Jew who will embrace Islam.

3. **A Jihad of Fear**: The death penalty for anyone leaving Islam for another religion.

4. **A Jihad of Slavery**: Black slavery is practiced even today in some Muslim countries. The capturing and selling of black women and children on a slave market.

5. **A Jihad of Sharia Law**: Non-Muslims living in Islamic lands are denied equal access in courts as well as denial of equal protection. The testimony in court of a non-Muslim is not valid against a Muslim.

George Braswell, in his book, "**What You Need to Know About Islam**," page 38, lists four Jihads of which have been modified and abbreviated in this text:

1. **Jihad of Speaking**: Speaking, talking about Islam, literally, a constant conversation to spread Islam.

2. **Jihad of Serving**: Doing good works, working in the community, acting as a good citizen.

3. **Jihad of Submission**: Being a good Muslim, living according to the Koran, Friday prayers, etc.

4. **Jihad of Sword**: Fighting, killing, or causing to submit to the rule of Islamic law and defending the Islamic faith, by committing jihad against non-Muslims (Christians and Jews).

Contrary to the politically correct crowds and the "useful idiots" of Islam, jihad is a very real war being waged in America and around the globe. C.A.I.R., which is an arm of the Muslim Brotherhood; a global Muslim movement is out to control the world. C.A.I.R. is active in almost every area of society attempting to bring about acceptance of Islam and its wicked ideologies. Often the media, politicians, the politically correct crowds and even some Christian denominations do not comprehend that they are being used by the Islamics as "useful idiots" to bring about the Muslim's agenda.

" O YOU WHO BELIEVE! <u>TAKE NOT THE JEWS AND THE CHRISTIANS AS FRIENDS;</u> THEY ARE BUT FRIENDS TO EACH OTHER. AND IF ANY AMONGST YOU TAKES THEM AS FRIENDS, THEN SURELY HE IS ONE OF THEM. VERILY ALLAH GUIDES NOT THOSE PEOPLE WHO ARE POLYTHEISTS AND WRONG-DOERS.

SURAH 5:51

22

Islam and CHRISTIAN FRIENDS

Are Muslims allowed to make friends with Christians, Jews or other non-Muslims? **The summary answer is no.** Unbelievers are described by Muhammad in the Koran as the vilest of animals and losers, all Muslims are commanded in the Koran to refuse friendship with Christians and Jews. If any Muslim denies this, they are either lying or they are ignorant of their own demonic book, the Koran. In most cases, the Muslim knows this as a fact, but will deceive to appease the hearer.

Christians and Jews are hated by Allah, according to the Koran, to the extent that they are destined for eternal doom as a result of their disbelief in Allah and Islam. It would make no sense for Muhammad to recommend them to be taken as friends by Muslims. In fact, the Koran plainly commands **all Muslims** not to take unbelievers (**non-Muslims**) as friends.

The Koran and Non-Muslim Friends

Surah 5:51 "O you who believe! <u>Take not the Jews and the Christians as friends;</u> they are but friends to each other. And if any amongst you takes them as friends, then surely he is one of them. Verily Allah guides not those people who are polytheists and wrongdoers."

Surah 5:80 "You will see many of them taking the disbelievers as friends. Evil indeed is that which their ownselves have sent forward before them; for that (reason) Allah's wrath fell upon them and in torment they will abide." <u>Those Muslims who befriend unbelievers will abide in Hell.</u>

Surah 3:28 "Let not the believers (Muslims) <u>take not disbelievers (non-Muslims) for friends or helpers</u> instead of the believers, and whoever does that will never be helped by Allah in any way, except indeed if you do fear a danger from them. And Allah warns you against himself (his punishment) and to Allah is the final return."

Surah 3:118 "o you who believe! <u>Take not as (your) (friends helpers, advisors, consultants, protectors), those outside your Religion (i.e. pagans, Jews, Christians,</u> and hypocrites) since they will not fail to do their best to corrupt you. They desire to harm you severely. Hatred has already appeared from their mouths, but what their breasts conceal is far worse..."

These Surahs not only warn Muslims not to take non-Muslims as friends, but it establishes the deep-seated rejection and hatred the Islamic world has toward America and the entire western world of which Islam views as Christian. Remember, America is called "the great Satan" by all of the Islamic nations.

Surah 9:23 "O you who believe! Take not as your (supporters and helpers) your fathers and your brothers if they prefer disbelief to belief. And whoever of you does so, then he is one of the wrong doers."

In this Surah, even family members are not to be taken as friends if they do not accept Islam, or they have left Islam. This is the mildest interpretation of this text from the 9th Surah, which also advocates slaying the unbelievers wherever you find them.

Surah 53:29 "Therefore withdraw (O Muhammad) from them who turns away from our reminder (this Koran) and desires nothing but the life of this world."

Surah 3:85 "And whoever seeks a religion other than Islam, it will never be accepted of him, and in the hereafter he shall be one of the losers."

Surah 3:10 "Verily, those who disbelieve, neither their properties nor their offspring will avail them whatsoever against Allah, and it is they who will be fuel of the fire."

Surah 7:44 "And the dwellers of Paradise will call out to the dwellers of the fire (saying) We have indeed found true what our Lord had promised us; have you also found true what your Lord promised (warnings)? They shall say; yes. Then a crier will proclaim between them: The curse of Allah is on the polytheists and wrong-doers."

Surah 1:5-7 "You alone we worship, and you alone we ask for help (for each and everything). Guide us to the straight way. The way of those on whom you have bestowed your grace not (the way) of those who earned your anger nor of those who went astray."

This is a prayer that Muslims are supposed to repeat each day. "Those who earn thine anger" specifically refer to Jews and "those who go astray" to refer to Christians.

Hadith and Non-Muslim Friends

Muslim 1:147 taken to mean that one's own relatives should not be taken as friends if they are not Muslim.

Bukhari 59:572 "o you who believe take not my enemies and your enemies as friends offering them your love even though they have disbelieved in that truth Allah prophet Muhammad and this Koran which has come to you."

Abu Dawud 41:4832 "The messenger of Allah said do not keep company with anyone but a believer and do not let anyone eat your food but one who is pious."

Other Teachings of Islam on Friendship with Christians

Even though they are explicitly kufr (unbelievers: Koran 5:17, 4:44-59), Jews and Christians are given special status in Islam. So, if Muhammad warned Muslims against taking them as friends, then it surely is not permissible for Muslims to befriend atheists or those of other religions, therefore <u>the reference would be to any and all who are not Islamic.</u>

Surah 5:17 "Surely, in disbelief are they who say that Allah is the Messiah, son of Maryam (Mary). Say (O Muhammad): "Who then has the least power against Allah, if He were to destroy the Messiah, son of Maryam (Mary), his mother, and all those who are on the earth together?" And to Allah belongs the dominion of the heavens and the earth, and all that is between them. He creates what He wills. And Allah is able to do all things."

Surah 4:44-59 "Have you not seen those who were given a portion of the book (the Jews), purchasing the wrong path, and wish that you should go astray from the Right Path? Allah has full knowledge of your enemies, and Allah is Sufficient as a Protector, and Allah is Sufficient as a Helper. Among those who are Jews, there are some who displace words from (their) right places and say: "We hear your word (O Muhammad) and disobey," and "Hear and let you (O Muhammad) hear nothing." And (listen) with a <u>twist of their tongues and as a mockery of the religion (Islam)</u>. And if only they had said: "We hear and obey", and "Do make us understand," it would have been better for them, (non-Muslims) and more proper, but <u>Allah has cursed them for their disbelief</u>, so they believe not except a few. O you who have been given the Scripture (Jews and Christians)! Believe in what We have revealed (to Muhammad) confirming what is (already) with you, before we efface faces (by making them like the back of necks; without nose, mouth, eyes) and turn them hindwards, or curse them as We cursed the Sabbath-breakers. And the Commandment of Allah is always executed. Verily, Allah forgives not that partners should be set up with him (in worship), but He forgives except that (anything else) to whom He wills, and whoever sets up partners with Allah in worship, he has indeed invented a tremendous sin. Have you not seen those (Jews and Christians) who claim sanctity for themselves. Nay, but Allah sanctifies whom He wills, and they will not be dealt with injustice even equal to the extent of a scalish thread in the long slit of a date-stone. Look, how they invent a lie against Allah, and enough is that as a manifest sin. <u>Have you not seen those who were given a portion of the Scripture? They (believe in false deities)</u> and say to the disbelievers that they are better guided as regards the way than the believers (Muslims). <u>They are those whom Allah has cursed, and he whom Allah curses, you will not find for him (any) helper.</u> Or have they a share in the dominion? Then in that case they would not give mankind even a speck on the back of a date-stone. Or do they envy men (Muhammad and his followers) for what Allah has given them of His Bounty? Then we had already given the family of Ibrâhim (Abraham) the Book and and (As-sunnah-Divine revelation to those prophets not written in the form of a book) conferred upon them a great kingdom. Of them were (some) who believed in him (Muhammad), and of them were (some) who averted their faces from him (Muhammad); and enough is Hell for burning (them). <u>Surely! Those who disbelieved (non-Muslims) in our proofs we shall burn them in Fire.</u> As often as their skins are roasted through, We shall change them for other skins that they may taste the punishment. Truly, Allah is Ever Most Powerful, All-Wise. But those who believe (Muslims) and do deeds of righteousness, Allah shall admit them to Paradise, abiding therein forever. Therein they shall have purified mates or wives (having no menses, stools, urine, etc.) and Allah shall admit them to shades wide and ever deepening (Paradise). Verily! Allah commands that you should render back the trusts to those whom they are due; and that when you judge between men, you judge with justice. Verily, how excellent is the teaching which Allah gives you! Truly, Allah is Ever All-Hearer, All-Seer. <u>O you who believe! Obey Allah and obey the Messenger (Muhammad), and those of you (Muslims) who are in authority.</u> (And) if you differ in anything amongst yourselves, refer it to Allah and His Messenger, if you believe in Allah and in the Last Day. That is better and more suitable for final determination."

Muslims interpret this to mean they **should not even act friendly towards non-Muslims** and warns Muslims against taking Christians as sincere friends. **Islam permits infidels (non-Muslims) to be dealt with in a kind manner only in the hope that they might become Muslims**. Otherwise, Muslims are forbidden to have any Christians or Jews as a friend.

Many Muslims are inwardly embarrassed by **Surah 5:51** and have gone to elaborate lengths to try to modify its intent or its impact by interpreting the word friend as 'guardian' or 'protector' which are just two of several other legitimate translations of the Arabic word. According to these apologists, the Surah is referring to a Muslim's allegiance to a non–Muslim government (which would also include the people).This however is refuted by the Surah itself, which distinguishes between <u>friends and protectors and instructs Muslims to avoid both.</u>

Surah 5:51 "O you who believe (Islam) take not the Jews and Christians as friends..."

Other Islamic apologists point to **Surah 60:8-9** which says that Allah doesn't necessarily forbid showing kindness to unbelievers , but to shun the ones who warred against you on account of religion, (reference to the Meccan's, whose leaders expelled Muhammad and his handful of followers from Mecca following his declaration of war against them). This Surah was given shortly after their arrival in Medina, when it was necessary for the Muslims to build alliances with non-Muslims in order to survive. **This was only until Muhammad had enough followers to fight the non-Muslims,** and force their submission or be killed. It is vital to <u>remember abrogation</u> of one Surah and replaced by another (see Chapter 3). <u>The Koran has "no context" to follow.</u>

Surah 60:8-9 "Allah does not forbid you to deal justly and kindly with those who fought not against you on account of religion and nor drove you out of your homes. Verily, Allah loves those who deal with equity. It is only as regards those who fought against you on account of religion, and have driven you out of your homes, and helped to drive you out, that Allah forbids you to befriend them. And whosoever will befriend them, then such are (the wrong-doers those who disobey Allah)."

The verse quoted from **Surah 9:5** <u>is given much later, when Muslims had power, and they expanded the scope of unfriendliness to include those who were not Muslim.</u>

Islam and Non-Muslim Marriage

Surah 5:5 "Made lawful to you this day [all kinds of halal (lawful)] foods which Allah has made lawful (meat of slaughtered eatable animals, milk products fats vegetables and fruits). The food (slaughtered cattle eatable animals) of the people of the Scripture (Jews and Christians) is lawful to you and yours is lawful to them. (Lawful to you in marriage) are chaste women from the believers and chaste women from these who were given the scripture, (Jews and Christians) before your time when you have given their bridal money given by marriage..."

In Islamic-Koranic law, the non-Muslim wife must become (convert to) Islam and follow all Islamic-Koranic laws of Islam. In another Surah in the Koran, it forbids Muslims from marrying Christians or Jews. If a marriage occurs, the Muslim husband must bring his family (wife and any children) into the Islamic religion.

Surah 2:221 "And do not marry (non-Muslims, idolatresses, etc.) till they believe (worship Allah alone). And indeed a slave woman who believes is better than a (free) non-Muslim woman even though she pleases you..."

Only Muslim men are allowed to marry outside of Islam. The women they marry must relinquish control over their own lives, even to the extent that they cannot raise their own child in any other religion or faith. All children and the wife may be beaten if she does not submit to Islam and the Koran. In recent years in America, some wives have been beheaded because the husband was not pleased with her.

This certainly doesn't sound like friendship to the non-Muslim. If your local Muslim advocate, leader or spokesperson tries to pretend otherwise, then simply ask if non-Muslim men may enter into this sort of friendship with a Muslim woman, then just listen and watch the double-talk and the Islamic deception.

Islam is very clear in teaching that there is no equality between Muslims and non-Muslims, and hence no basis for a relationship or friendship. Those who do not profess does not preclude Muslims from acting toward those who do. This does not preclude Muslims from acting friendly to others, of course but this does not constitute friendship as it is generally understood in the modern world. <u>In Islamic ideology, any outward gesture of friendship is exercised only to win over the non-Muslim to Islamic ideology and teachings,</u> (i.e.) believe and accept Islam as an authentic religion rather than a demonic system of hatred, murder, terrorism and despicable actions. Keep in mind a Muslim is authorized by the teachings of the Koran to lie when it is needful to cause another to believe him or accept his answer or reasoning on a subject or matter in dispute.

ISLAM DOES NOT BELIEVE IN
DIALOGUE; THEIR KORAN IS
THEIR FINAL WORD.

23

Islam and **DIALOGUE**

Religious freedom is not exactly a hallmark of Muslims or any Islamic countries. One of the most disconcerting features of Islam is the way "apostates" are treated. In Islam, those who choose to leave the faith are regarded as traitors, and death is the penalty, according to the Koran. Thus, there is no religious freedom, or dialogue to choose or decide independently. To receive Jesus Christ as savior is sure death or banishment.

Islam appears to be alone among the major world religions in their harsh and barbaric practice. Religious freedom and freedom of conscience are features of free and democratic nations. Indeed, Article 18 of the United Nations Universal Declaration of Human Rights states that **"Everyone has the right to freedom of thought, conscience and religion; this right includes freedom to change his religion or belief**." Freedom is the very bed-rock of our American Constitution; freedom of speech, religion and place of worship. We should thank God every day for our founding fathers and founding documents that codify the freedoms God himself has granted to man.

Islam does not have dialogue on any Muslim position as directed in the Koran. They reject the American Constitution and the Declaration of Independence. Though Islam declares that Christians and Jews should be willing to have dialogue, the facts are that Islamics will not dialogue on the vital points of the Koran and Sharia Law. Any attempt at serious questions, a Muslim will respond that you just don't understand or that you are a bigot. The goal of Islam is world domination, either by conversion or by jihad.

We begin by examining the Koran, the Hadith, and Sharia law. All three give approval for the punishment, harassment, and even death of those who dare to leave Islam or speak anything against the Koran or Muhammad, even a cartoon of Muhammad. In the Koran, are a number of passages which speak of severe punishment for those who oppose Islam.

Surah 2:217 "They ask you concerning fighting in the sacred months (i.e. 1st 7th 11th and 12th months of the Islamic calendar). Say 'fighting therein is a great (transgression), but a greater (transgression) with Allah is to prevent mankind from following the way of Allah, to disbelieve in him, to prevent access to Al-masjid −Al-haram (at Mecca) and to drive out its inhabitants, and Al-Fitnah is worse than killing.' They will never cease fighting you until they turn you back from your religion if they can. And whosoever of you turns back from his religion and dies as a disbeliever, then his deeds will be lost in this life and the hereafter, and they will be the dwellers of the fire. They will abide therein forever."

Surah 16:106 "Whoever disbelieved in Allah after his belief, except him who is forced thereto and whose heart is at rest with Faith: but such as open their breasts to disbelief, on them is wrath from Allah, and theirs will be a great torment."

Surah 88:24 "Then Allah will punish him with the greatest punishment."

Many Muslim jurists, commentators and scholars who favor this reading of the Koran, say that it is the correct interpretation. An examination of the Hadith, and provisions in Sharia law will be noted. For example, Muhammad is cited in Bukhari as saying:

> **"Whoever changed his [Islamic] religion, then kill him."**

As to the Islamic legal code, the different schools are fairly uniform when it comes to the Islamic apostasy law. All prescribe the death penalty for apostasy, and each one states that rulers or their deputies can only carry out the punishment. Yet they also say that **if an individual kills an apostate, he is not to be punished in any way**. Modern Muslim scholars and jurists on this issue demonstrate the clear linkage between apostasy, heresy and blasphemy.

271

These last two crimes are also considered to be severe, and should also be punished by death. **Simply put, Islam has no interest in dialogue when it comes to their stand on the Koran and its teachings.** NO dialogue about the authenticity of the Holy Bible and its teachings, NO dialogue about Jesus being Holy God, or the teachings of the Trinity, **"NO DIALOGUE."** This contrasts Islam with the Judeo-Christian tradition when it comes to human rights.

Muslims regard Islam and the community as paramount, and do not have a high regard or recognition of autonomous, individual rights. Indeed, the former are always to trump the latter. Thus, in a few Muslim nations, you will find both Sharia law and various forms of Western secular law existing together. **However, it is Sharia law which determines if and when human rights and equality can be allowed.** France, Germany, The United Kingdom, Canada and many other nations are conceding to allow some form of Sharia law to please the Muslims. The United States, via the State Department and the Department of Finance have already developed a division of Sharia Finance. Part of the financial bail-out package went to A.I.G., which has major holdings in Sharia Finance. In October 2010, a New Jersey court ruled that a Muslim man could beat and rape his wife because the Koran approves this activity.

While not every Muslim nation carries out the death penalty for apostasy (the main ones are Saudi Arabia, North Sudan, Iran, Afghanistan, Pakistan, Mauritania and Yemen and much of Islamic Africa), death can still result, since laws against treason can also be invoked, and they too mandate the sentence of death. **Therefore all other Muslim countries will carry out the death penalty whenever possible on trumped-up charges of treason.** Elsewhere, a sort of living death will be experienced by converts out of Islam. They will be severely punished, harassed and mistreated in various ways for their defection. Social ostracism, dismissal from jobs, beatings, dismemberment and general second-class citizenship (*dhimmitude*) are all part of the daily reality for non-Muslims and many ex-Muslims. There is a death warrant out on the life of The Son of Hamas, a former Muslim from Israel, who wrote a book entitled, "**Son of Hamas**," because he converted to Christianity (he now lives in America, as a refugee). He lives in the shadows because a death warrant has been issued on his life. "**NO DIALOGUE**."

Muslims are seeking to gain a privileged position in this regard on the international level. The 57-member nations of the Organization of the Islamic Conference (OIC) have been heavily lobbying the UN and EU, for example, to get preferential treatment, so that Islam can continue doing business as usual. President Obama just directed the head of NASA to contract the space program to Indonesia to create a better relationship with Islam. Islam has pushed the UN General Assembly and other UN bodies to adopt resolutions which seek to prevent any negative criticism of Islam, something accorded to no other major religion. The "OIC is seeking international legitimization of its own state-sanctioned blasphemy laws." **Under the Presidential directives in Washington, terrorism is not to be referred to as "Islamic terrorism."** Wake up America, <u>we may have a Muslim president.</u>

Islam does not want, seek or desire dialogue. A good example of this is that on 10/20/2010, National Public Radio fired journalist Juan Williams as a result of C.A.I.R.'s demand that they fire Williams. Juan Williams made the mistake, according to C.A.I.R.'s Ibrahim Hooper (Spokesperson), that Williams should not have questioned or discussed Islam's role in the 9/11 attack on America, which resulted in his (Williams) concern when he sees a person dressed in Muslim garb get on an airplane. C.A.I.R./Islam is not interested in debate, dialogue or discussion on the merits of free speech or the rights of honest U.S. Citizens. Islam is demanding preferential treatment. The frightening thing is that the liberal media are being used as Islam's "useful idiots" to promote the Islamic agenda of domination and control through the implementation of Sharia Law in America.

Should these trends continue, there will be no need in the future for *fatwas (decrees)* such as those issued by

Ayatollah Khomeini demanding the death of Salmon Rushdie. Non-Muslim states will themselves prosecute their own citizens for alleged 'blasphemy,' or 'hate speech' against Muhammad and Islam. Indeed, this is already happening around the world. Islamic activists pronounce the 21st century as the century for Global control by Islam. As Islam increases in any nation, terrorism, honor killings and Sharia law become a reality. U.S. Supreme Court Justice Breyer recently said that there should be a law to prevent any negative statements about Islam.

Theological pluralism prevailed throughout America in the early nineteenth century. Because of the American embrace of and allowance of other religions, Christianity is now being demeaned, marginalized and minusculized as only one of many religions. As a result of the low view of Christianity held by Islam and the politically correct masses, we are now in a position of having to defend Christianity while Washington D.C. and the politicians defend, protect and excuse the Islamic Jihadist in America. Our president, Barak Hussein Obama authorizes millions for what he calls "outreach to Muslims."

Although it is being kept under the radar by the F.B.I. and law enforcement in general, Islamic honor killing is on a rapid increase in America. Honor killing, the practice of the Father, Brother or other family male figure killing the Wife, or Daughter for what they call "dishonoring the family," by being raped, having a non-Muslim boyfriend, going out in public with their face uncovered, or being seen with a man that is not the Husband or other family member.All of this is practiced under Islamic Sharia Law or Koranic Law.

Imam Feisal Abdul Rauf, the Ground Zero Mosque leader does not believe in religious dialogue, yet he publically says that the mosque program in New York will enhance and encourage inter-faith dialogue. Rauf said, "**The only law that the Muslim needs exists already in the Koran and the Hadith**." Rauf believes that Sharia law must be the rule of every nation around the globe. Thus, honor killing, jihad and all other commands of the Koran are to be the global rule.

24

Islam - QUOTES

- "The prophet Muhammad was a terrorist and a violent man of war."

  Dr. Jerry Falwell, Pastor
  Thomas Road Baptist Church

- "Islam is a very wicked and evil, religion."

  Rev. Franklin Graham, Evangelist

- "Ever since the religion of Islam appeared in the world, espousers of it...have been as wolves and tigers to all other nations, rending and tearing all that fell into their merciless paws, and grinding them with their iron teeth."

  John Wesley (1703-1791)
  Methodist Leader

- "Islam is wicked, evil and very dangerous."

  Dr. Pat Robertson, CBN Broadcast

- "This is an Islamic crusade against America."

  President G.W. Bush (After 9-11 attacks)

- "Islam is the most dangerous, wicked, destructive religion in the world."

   Dr. Gene A. Youngblood, Founder/President Conservative Theological University

- "Muhammad was a demon-possessed pedophile."

   Dr. Jerry Vines, Former Pres. Southern Baptist Convention

- "Islam is evil, very, very evil, wicked; very dangerous."

   Dr. Mark Gabriel
   Former Professor of Islamic Studies, Al-Azhar University, Cairo, Egypt

- "The Pentagon's politically correct, wouldn't recognize a Muslim terrorist if one jumped up and bit them on the butt."

   Jim O'Neill

- "Today [1950], the hatred of the Muslim countries against the West is becoming hatred against Christianity itself."

   Fulton J. Sheen (1895-1979)
   Renowned Catholic Bishop

- "Jihad is for liberation of all Muslims around the world. When we succeed in this part, we will move to other parts until we ensure only Allah is worshipped in this world."

   Sheikh Ali Dhere,
   Al Shabaab spokesman

- "Bolshevism combines the characteristics of the French Revolution with those of the rise of Islam…Mohammadism and Bolshevism are practical, social, unspiritual, concerned to win the empire of this world."

  Bertrand Russell (1872-1970)
  Liberal Icon

- "Just as the Jews ran from Gaza, the Americans will run from Iraq and Afghanistan and the Russians will run from Chechnya, and the Indians will run from Kashmir, and our prisoners will be released from Guantanamo. The prisoners will be released by Allah's will, not by peaceful means and not by agreements, but they will be released by the sword, they will be released by the gun, this is the Jihad of Allah."

  Al-Qassam Brigades
  Media Office 6/3/2006

- "The Koran is a fascist book which promotes violence and is similar to Adolf Hitler's "**Mein Kampf**." The Koran should be banned, outlawed for use in the Mosque and at home."

  Geert Wilder
  Radio Netherlands Worldwide, 8/9/2007

- "How dreadful are the curses which Muhammadism lays on its votaries! Individual Muslims may show splendid qualities—but the influence of the religion paralyses the social development of those who follow it. No stronger retrograde force exists in this world."

  Sir Winston Churchill (1874-1965)
  British Prime Minister

- "Adopting from the new Revelation of Jesus, the faith and the hope of immortal life, and of future retribution, he [Mohammad] humbled it to the dust by adapting all the rewards and sanctions of his religion to the gratification of the sexual passion...and he declared undistinguishing and exterminating war, as part of his religion, against all the rest of mankind. THE ESSENCE OF HIS DOCTRINE WAS VIOLENCE AND LUST.—TO EXALT THE BRUTAL OVER THE SPIRITUAL PART OF HUMAN NATURE...The war is yet flagrant...while merciless and dissolute dogmas of the false prophet shall furnish motives to human action, there can never be peace upon the earth, and good will towards men."

  John Quincy Adams (1767-1848)
  Sixth President of the United States

- "C.A.I.R.'s modus operandi has been to attack Christianity with the same simplistic broad brush it claims is tarring Islam."

  Bob Jones, World Magazine 3/22/2003

- "Fighting for freedom, fighting for Islam, that is not suicide, they kill themselves for Islam."

  Omar M. Ahmad, C.A.I.R. Chairman

- "Governors and political institutions should consult Muslim religious institutions and Muslim personalities in the field so as to assure their decision-making to reflect the spirit of Sharia," (Islamic Koranic law)."

  Abdul Rauf
  Ground Zero Imam

- Council on American Islamic Relations (C.A.I.R.) is an extremist organization –founder Omar Ahmad's 1998 assertion "that Islam must one day dominate the U.S."—the newspaper, the **Fremont Argus in California** continues to stand by its story. The reporter **Lisa Gardiner**, along with the editor, **Steve Waterhouse**, who says he is sure "that she got it right." 1998 Argus Article, also published in the sister newspaper **San Ramon Valley Herald**, paraphrased **Ahmad** saying, "Islam isn't in America to be equal to any other faith, but to become dominant, and the Koran, the Muslim book of Scripture, should be the highest authority in America, and Islam the only accepted religion on Earth."

  Lisa Gardiner, Reporter, Fremont Argus

- "The Muslim Brotherhood and Hamas from which C.A.I.R. is derived have affirmed the traditional Islamic notion that the law of Islam must be ultimately imposed by Muslims."

  Robert Spencer, Director of Jihad Watch

- "Islam is a religion in which god requires you to send your son to die for him. Christianity is a faith in which God sends His son to die for you."

  John Ashcroft
  U.S. Attorney General 2001-2005

- "(The Koran) provides ample evidence that Islam encourages violence in order to win converts and to reach the ultimate goal of an Islamic world."

  Rev. Franklin Graham

- Internal Hamas documents strongly suggest that parts of the Hamas charter ...were first written by members of the I.A.P. (Islamic Association for Palestine) in the United States in the early to mid-1980's...The IAP has a long history of links to the Middle East terrorism and its financial support..."

  > Steven Emerson, Investigational Journalist
  > Testimony to Senate Judiciary,
  > Sub-Committee on Terrorism, Technology
  > and Government Information

- "Omar M. Ahmad, chairman of the board of the Council on American Islamic Relations, spoke before a packed crowd at the Flamingo Palace banquet hall on Peralta Boulevard, urging Muslims not to shirk their duty of sharing Islamic faith with those who are 'on the wrong side.' Muslim institutions, schools and economic power should be strengthened in America. If you choose to live here in America, you have a responsibility to deliver the message of Islam. Islam isn't in America to be equal to any other faith, but to become dominant. The Koran, the Muslim book of scripture, should be the highest authority in America, and Islam the only acceptable religion on Earth."

  > Feraidoon Mojadedi
  > 1998 Director of Islamic Study School

- "I wouldn't want to create the impression that I wouldn't like the government of the United States to be Islamic sometime in the future, but I'm not going to do anything violent to promote that. I'm going to do it through education."

  > Ibrahim Hooper, C.A.I.R. Spokesperson

- "I don't hate Muslims, I just hate their false doctrines."

  Rev. Creighton Lovelace, Pastor
  Danieltown Baptist Church, NC

- "What we are witnessing here are hate crimes against Christianity."

  Pat Buchanan, Commentator

- "If you don't want a Christian nation, then go to the many nations that are heathen already, rather than perverting ours. You're welcome to come, but leave your religions, your bibles, all your other things back where you came from. Islam and America are opposites. They hate us. They want to kill us."

  Rev. Jeff Fugate, Pastor
  Clays Mills Rd. Baptist Church, KY

- "The size and nature of Britain's Muslim population presents a threat to national security."

  Professor David Voas
  Manchester University

- "Islamization of a nation begins where there are sufficient Muslims in a country to agitate (push, demand) for their religious rights."

  Free Republic, 2/5/2010

- "Muhammad; an illiterate barbarian."

  Gibbons, "The Decline and Fall of the Roman Empire, Vol.2" pg. 657

- "I have many Muslim friends, but I want the people of this country to know that the god of Islam is not the Christian God. The god of Islam is not a father. The God of Christianity was the father of Jesus Christ... This country was not built by Hindus, nor Muslims, nor Atheists. It was built by Christian men and women...But where are the Muslim Clerics? When people say this is a "peaceful religion," don't tell me that. When a suicide bomber straps on a bomb, that's not peaceful."

  Rev. Franklin Graham

- "My heart sank when they opened the National Day of Prayer and Remembrance service in the name of God, Abraham, Isaac, Jacob, Jesus and Allah. I don't pray in the name of Ba'al any more than I pray in the name of Allah. Because guess what? Allah is a different god. It's not one big umbrella and we shouldn't just get along. If you look at the Bible, God isn't real fond of people who pray to false gods.

  Janet Folger, head of the Center for
  Reclaiming America

- "If I had stayed in Ohio, I wouldn't be alive. In 150 generations in my family, no one has ever known Jesus. I am the first; imagine the (Muslims) honor in killing me."

  Rifqa Bary, 17 year old former Muslim,
  Now a Christian

- "I believe Muslims are dangerous."

  Lou Ann Zelenik, GOP
  Congressional Candidate

- "Islam is not just a belief; it is a way of life, a violent way of life. Islam is imbued with violence and it encourages violence...Strict interpretation of Islam is preparation for bigotry, violence and oppression...It is part of Muslim culture to oppress women...There is no counter to the propaganda that the jihadists offer."

  Ayaan Hirsi Ali, Author
  "From Islam to America"

- "Somebody may say: 'Do you want to deny freedom to people?' We say to him: 'If what is meant by freedom is to disbelieve in Allah's religion or the freedom of infidelity and apostasy (leaving Islam), then that freedom is abolished and we do not recognize it; we even call for its eradication, and we strive to oppress it.' We declare that publicly and in daylight."

  Dr. Taha Jabir
  "The Islamic Society," pg. 26

- "When I began to study the Koran, the holy book of Islam, I found many unreasonable ideas. The women in the Koran were treated as slaves. They are nothing but sexual objects. Naturally I set aside the Koran and looked around me. I found religion equally oppressive in real life. And I realized that religious oppression and injustices are only increasing, especially in Muslim countries. The religious terrorists are everywhere.

  Taslima Nasrin
  Bangladeshi writer in exile

- "The Koran is a dangerous book; it should be banned in America."

  Mosab Hassan Yousef, Son of Hamas

- "The deeper study of the Koran, Hadith and Arab history led me to believe that Islam has been cleverly devised on the principle of divide and rule. And its purpose is to enable the Arabs to dominate the rest of the world."

  Anwar Shaikh

- "A religion of peace? You can't say that Islam is a religion of peace because Islam does not mean peace. It means submission. So the Muslim is the one who submits. There is a place for violence in Islam. There is a place for Jihad in Islam."

  Anjem Choudary
  Muslim leader in U.K.

- "Muslims are waging civil war against us, an undeclared "intifada" against the police with violent clashes injuring an average of 14 officers each day...We are in a state of civil war orchestrated by Islamists. This is not a question of urban violence any more, it is an 'intifada:" We need armored vehicles and water cannons. They are the only things that will disperse crowds of hundreds of people (Muslims) trying to kill us."

  Nicolas Sarkozy, Interior Minister, France

- "But it's undeniable that there's a portion of Islam that's been co-opted by a radical faction that promotes violence, not only against Americans, but around the world."

  Ron Ramsey, Tenn. Lt. Gov.

- "...Every honest informed Muslim knows very well what America would be like if it were under Islamic rule. It would be a hell on earth with only **inhuman rights**..."

  Henry R. Pike, PhD.
  "What is the Religion of Islam", pg. 7

- "I opened the Koran and smelled a stinking, bloated, dead rat on every page."

  Rev. Marc Morte, Pastor
  Faith Baptist Church, Avon, IN
  World Net Daily 9/9/2003

- "I am all about freedom of religion, but they cross the line when they start trying to bring Sharia law into the United States. Now you could even argue whether being a Muslim is actually a religion, or is it a nationality, a way of life or cult, whatever you want to call it? We do protect our religions, but at the same time, this is something we will have to face."

  Ron Ramsey, Tenn. Lt. Gov.

- "The only law that the Muslim needs exists already in the Koran and Hadith."

  Abdul Rauf
  Ground Zero Imam

- "Governments that want to ensure the new laws as to not contradict Sharia rules, so they create institutions to ensure Islamic law and remove any that contradict with Sharia."

  Abdul Rauf, Ground Zero Imam

- "Two Christians, a pastor and his brother were murdered. Authorities report 36-year old Rashid Emmanuel and his brother, Sajid, 30, were shot and killed on the Faisalabad courthouse steps...They had been taken there on accusations of blaspheming Muhammad...Two Christians were shot and killed on their way from a courthouse to jail after being accused by Pakistani Muslims of blasphemy...If a Christian is accused of blasphemy, even if the Christian has not done it, and even the police have proved that the person hasn't done it, it doesn't matter for them...Intelligence analyst Bill Warner, who heads the Center for the Study of Political Islam, says he's not surprised by the shootings. 'The killing of a blasphemer is pure Sharia, the perfect example of Muhammad', Warner observed."

  World Net Daily 7/22/2010

- "Responding to France's ban of the Islamic veil, the new head of the Muslim Brotherhood asserted Islam ultimately will triumph over the United States and Europe...I have complete faith that Islam will invade Europe and America, because Islam had logic and a mission," said Muhammad Mahdi Othman' Akef (head of the Muslim Brotherhood).

  WorldNet Daily Article 2/4/2004

- "Jihad is physically fighting the enemies of Islam to protect and advance the religion of Islam. This is Jihad."

  Zaid Shakir, Islamic Cleric
  Speaker at C.A.I.R. events
  WND article 5/7/2010

- "The mistake the westerners make when they think about Islam is that they impose their own views of religion onto something decidedly outside Western tradition. Because violence is done in the name of God is extreme from a Western/Christian point of view, they imagine that it must be so from an Islamic one. But unlike Christianity, which recognizes a separate sphere for secular politics ("Render unto Caesar what is Caesar's and unto God what is God's) Islam has never distinguished between faith and power. While Christianity is doctrinally concerned primarily with the salvation of souls, Islam seeks to remake the world in its image. According to orthodox Islam, Sharia Law—the codified commandments of the Koran and precedents of the Prophet Muhammad—is the only legitimate basis of government. Islam is in fact an expansionary social and political system more akin to national socialism and communism than any "religion" familiar to Westerners. Islamic politics is inevitably an all-or-nothing affair in which the stakes are salvation or damnation and the aim is to not beat one's opponent at the polls but to destroy him—literally as well as politically."

  Gordon M. Davis, Ph.D.Author, "Religion of Peace?...Islam's War Against the World"

- "We've closed our eyes for far too long."

  Reza Safa, author,
  "Inside Islam"

- Asked whether such a global religious war would be "Islam vs. Christianity and Judaism combined," Lieberman, an orthodox Jew said, "Islam against fanatical Islam against Christianity, Judaism, Hinduism, every other –ism, every other religion, including Islam that doesn't agree with these fanatics…This is a battle to stop al-Qaida, Saddam Hussein and every other enemy of freedom and modernity from turning the beginning of the 21st century into what is truly unbelievable, which would be a global religious war."

    Joe Lieberman, Senator (Dem.) CT
    Interview with Associated Press, 11/30/2003

- "Islamic radicals are being trained at terrorist camps in Pakistan and Kashmir as part of a conspiracy to send hundreds of operatives to "sleeper cells" in the United States according to the U.S. and foreign officials. Al-Qaeda sleeper cells are believed to be operating in 40 states, according to F.B.I. and other federal authorities, awaiting orders and funding for new attacks in the United States."

    Jerry Seper, Washington Times, 2/10/2004

- Predicting "The imminent defeat of the United States of America at the hands of Muslim forces," "Consider me only a first droplet of the flood that will follow me." "If I am given 1,000 lives, I will sacrifice them all for the sake of Allah."

    Convicted Times Square Bomber,
    Faisal Shazad
    10/6/2010

- "Ohio authorities are investigating youth pastor Brian Williams for his assistance of Rifqa Bary, 17, who claimed she fled her Muslim parents last year because her father threatened to kill her after learning she had become a Christian...I think this is another aspect of Islamic warfare that's going on, attempting to intimidate people into staying away from anything that may be considered a criticism of Islam...You can take action to save someone from harm. If you believe someone is in harm's way, you can take action to help...I am astonished the police and prosecutors have gone so far as to continue to go after Brian Williams...If you take seriously that apostates can be killed and have been killed, then it just doesn't make any sense that American law enforcement is investigating a youth minister who was acting basically to save a life...What kind of nation what kind of society are we living in where someone who helps a girl whose life is in danger is prosecuted for it? An Islamic one...A World Net Daily source said Bary now has been declared a dependent of the state of Ohio...Scholars in all the major streams of Islam have asserted the religion's holy book, the Koran, teaches that rejection of Islam must be punished by death."

World Net Daily Article 3/12/2010

- "Allah is our god; the prophet is our guide; the Koran is our Constitution; Jihad is our way; and death for the glory of Allah is our greatest ambition."

Muslim Brotherhood Credo,
Pg. 227, "**Muslim Mafia**,"
by David Gaubatz

- "Last month I attended my annual training session that's required for maintaining my state prison security clearance. During the training session there was a presentation by three speakers representing the Roman Catholic, Protestant and Muslim faiths who explained their belief systems. I was particularly interested in what the Islamic Imam had to say. The Imam gave a great presentation of the basics of Islam, complete with a video...I directed my questions to the Imam and asked, "Please, correct me if I am wrong, but I understand that most Imams and clerics of Islam have declared holy jihad (holy war) against the infidels of the world. And, that by killing an infidel, which is a command to all Muslims, they are assured of a place in Heaven. If that's the case, can you give me the definition of an infidel?" There was no disagreement with my statements and without hesitation he replied, "Nonbelievers!" I responded, "All followers of Allah have been commanded to kill everyone who is not of your faith so they can go to heaven, is that correct?" The expression on his face changed from one of authority and command to that of a little boy who had just gotten caught with his hand in the cookie jar. He sheepishly replied, 'Yes.'"

  Rick Mathes, well-known Prison Ministry Leader, 1/7/2004

25

Islam – Geert Wilder's Open Plea

Recently, the Brits tried to keep Wilder from speaking in England. The reasoning was political correctness and concern for Muslim "sensitivities."

Here is the speech of Geert Wilder, Chairman, Party for Freedom, the Netherlands, at the Four Seasons Hotel in New York, where he was introducing an Alliance of Patriots and announcing the coming Jihad Conference in Jerusalem.

Dear friends,

Thank you very much for inviting me.

I come to America with a mission. All is not well in the old world. There is a tremendous danger looming, and it is very difficult to be optimistic. We might be in the final stages of the Islamization of Europe. This not only is a clear and present danger to the future of Europe itself, it is a threat to America and the sheer survival of the West. The United States is the last bastion of Western civilization, facing an Islamic Europe.

First, I will describe the situation on the ground in Europe. Then, I will say a few things about Islam. To close, I will tell you about a meeting in Jerusalem.

The Europe you know is changing. You have probably seen the landmarks. But in all of these cities, sometimes a few blocks away from your tourist destination, there is another world. It is the world of the parallel society created by Muslim mass-migration.

All throughout Europe, a new reality is rising: entire Muslim neighborhoods where very few indigenous people reside or are even seen. And if they are (seen), they might regret it. This goes for the police as well. It's the world of head scarves, where women walk around in figureless tents, with baby strollers and a group of children. Their husbands, or slave holders, if you prefer, walk three steps ahead. With mosques on many street corners and the shops have signs you and I cannot read. You will be hard-pressed to find any economic activity. These are Muslim ghettos controlled by religious fanatics. These are Muslim neighborhoods, and they are mushrooming in every city across Europe. These are the building-blocks for territorial control of increasingly larger portions of Europe, street by street, neighborhood by neighborhood, city by city.

There are now thousands of mosques throughout Europe, with larger congregations than there are in churches. In every European city, there are plans to build super-mosques that will dwarf every church in the region. Clearly, the signal is: we rule (meaning Muslims).

Many European cities are already one-quarter Muslim: just take Amsterdam, (Netherlands) Marseille (France), and Malmo, in Sweden. In many cities, the majority of the under-18 population is Muslim. Paris is now surrounded by a ring of Muslim neighborhoods. Mohammed is the most popular name among boys in many cities.

In some elementary schools in Amsterdam, the farm can no longer be mentioned, because that would also mean mentioning the pig, and that would be an insult to Muslims.

Many state schools in Belgium and Denmark only serve halal food to all pupils. In once-tolerant Amsterdam, gays are beaten up almost exclusively by Muslims. Non-Muslim women routinely hear 'whore, whore'. Satellite dishes are not pointed to local TV stations, but to stations in the country of origin.

In France, school teachers are advised to avoid authors deemed offensive to Muslims, including Voltaire and Diderot; the same is increasingly true of Darwin. The history of the Holocaust can no longer be taught because of Muslim sensitivity.

In England, Sharia courts are now officially part of the British legal system. Many neighborhoods in France are no-go areas for women without head scarves. Last week, a man almost died after being beaten up by Muslims in Brussels, because he was drinking during the Ramadan.

Jews are fleeing France in record numbers, on the run for the worst wave of anti-Semitism since World War II. French is now commonly spoken on the streets of Tel Aviv and Netanya, Israel. I could go on forever with stories like this. Stories about Islamization.

A total of fifty-four million Muslims now live in Europe. San Diego University recently calculated that a staggering 25 percent of the population in Europe will be Muslim just 12 years from now. Bernhard Lewis has predicted a Muslim majority by the end of this century.

Now these are just numbers, and the numbers would not be threatening if the Muslim immigrants had a strong desire to assimilate. But there are few signs of that. The

Pew Research Center reported that half of French Muslims see their loyalty to Islam as greater than their loyalty to France. One-third of French Muslims do not object to suicide attacks. The British Centre for Social Cohesion reported that one-third of British Muslim students are in favor of a worldwide caliphate. Muslims demand what they call 'respect' and this is how we give them respect. We have Muslim official state holidays.

The Christian-Democratic Attorney General is willing to accept Sharia in the Netherlands, if there is a Muslim majority. We have cabinet members with passports from Morocco and Turkey.

Muslim demands are supported by unlawful behavior, ranging from petty crimes and random violence, for example, against ambulance workers and bus drivers, to small-scale riots. Paris has seen its uprising in the low-income suburbs, the banlieus. I call the perpetrators 'settlers' because that is what they are. They do not come to integrate into our societies; they come to integrate our society into their Dar-al-Islam. Therefore, they are settlers.

Much of this street violence I mentioned is directed exclusively against non-Muslims, forcing many native people to leave their neighborhoods, their cities, their countries. Moreover, Muslims are now a swing vote not to be ignored.

The second thing you need to know is the importance of Mohammed the prophet. His behavior is an example to all Muslims and cannot be criticized. Now, if Mohammed had been a man of peace, let us say like Ghandi and Mother Theresa wrapped in one, there would be no problem. But Muhammed was a warlord, a mass-murderer, a pedophile, and had several marriages - at the same time. Islamic tradition tells us how he fought in battles, how he had his enemies murdered and even had prisoners of war executed. Muhammed himself slaughtered the Jewish tribe of Banu Qurayza. If it is good for Islam, it is good. If it is bad for Islam, it is bad.

Let no one fool you about Islam being a religion. Sure, it has a god, and a here-after, and 72 virgins, but in its essence, Islam is a political ideology. It is a system that lays down detailed rules for society and the life of every person. Islam wants to dictate every aspect of life. Islam means 'submission'. Islam is not compatible with freedom and democracy, because what it strives for is Sharia. If you want to compare Islam to anything, compare it to communism or national-socialism, these are all totalitarian ideologies.

Now you know why Winston Churchill called Islam 'the most retrograde force in the world', and why he compared Mein Kampf to the Quran. The public has wholeheartedly accepted the Palestinian narrative, and sees Israel as the aggressor. I have lived in this country and visited it dozens of times. I support Israel. First, because it is the Jewish homeland after two thousand years of exile up to and including Auschwitz, second because it is a democracy, and third because Israel is our first line of defense.

This tiny country is situated on the fault line of jihad, frustrating Islam's territorial advance. Israel is facing the front lines of jihad, like Kashmir, Kosovo, the Philippines, Southern Thailand, Darfur in Sudan, Lebanon, and Aceh in Indonesia. Israel is simply in the way. The same way West Berlin was during the Cold War.

The war against Israel is not a war against Israel. It is a war against the West. It is jihad. Israel is simply receiving the blows that are meant for all of us. If there would have been no Israel, Islamic imperialism would have found other venues to release its energy and its desire for conquest. Thanks to Israeli parents who send their children to the army and lay awake at night, parents in Europe and America can sleep well and dream, unaware of the dangers looming.

Many in Europe argue in favor of abandoning Israel in order to address the grievances of our Muslim minorities. But if Israel were, God forbid, to go down, it would not bring any solace to the West. It would not mean our Muslim minorities would all of a sudden change their behavior, and accept our values. On the contrary, the end of Israel would give enormous encouragement to the forces of Islam. They would, and rightly so, see the demise of Israel as proof that the West is weak, and doomed. The end of Israel would not mean the end of our problems with Islam, but only the beginning. It would mean the start of the final battle for world domination. If they can get Israel, they can get everything. So-called journalists volunteer to label any and all critics of Islamization as a 'right-wing extremists' or 'racists'. In my country, the Netherlands, 60 percent of the population now sees the mass immigration of Muslims as the number one policy mistake since World War II. And another 60 percent sees Islam as the biggest threat. Yet, there is a greater danger than terrorist attacks, the scenario of America as the last man standing. The lights may go out in Europe faster than you can imagine. An Islamic Europe means a Europe without freedom and democracy, an economic wasteland, an intellectual nightmare, and a loss of military might for America - as its allies will turn into enemies, enemies with atomic bombs. With an Islamic Europe, it would be up to America alone to preserve the heritage of Rome, Athens and Jerusalem.

Dear friends, liberty is the most precious of gifts. My generation never had to fight for this freedom, it was offered to us on a silver platter, by people who fought for it with their lives. All throughout Europe, American cemeteries remind us of the young boys who never made it home, and whose memory we cherish. My generation does not own this freedom; we are merely its custodians. We can only hand over this hard won liberty to Europe's children in the same state in which it was offered to us. We cannot strike a deal with Mullahs and Imams. Future generations would never forgive us. We cannot squander our liberties. We simply do not have the right to do so. We have to take the necessary action now to stop this Islamic stupidity from destroying the free world that we know.

IF THIS BOOK HAS INFORMED, EDUCATED, AND ENLIGHTENED YOU...PAUSE AND PRAY FOR AMERICA AND SECURE AN EXTRA COPY OF THIS BOOK AND GIVE IT TO A FRIEND.

Conclusion

This book was written to advance the understanding of Islam and to sound the alarm as the reader is informed of the extreme dangers facing our nation from the Islamic invasion of America. It is my prayer that this book will provoke every patriot to action. We continue to see local, state and national political leaders turn a deaf ear toward any warnings. Rather than heeding the warnings, it seems as though the general attitude on every political level is that of appeasement for Islamic causes, and surrender to Muslim demands.

September 2010, U.S. Supreme Court Justice Steven Breyer compared burning the Koran to shouting "fire" in a crowded theater. Breyer's logic would suggest that some Islamists would riot and kill people after copies of the Koran were publically burned, therefore, we may need to outlaw Koran burning.

This would mean that Americans would be prohibited by law from expressing opinions against Islam. Breyer, the socialist, progressive, liberal that he is— suggests that since the internet makes it possible for news to instantly travel around the globe, the world is more dangerous by Americans simply showing descent or expressing themselves in ways which jihadist-Islamists react violently, therefore the courts should reinterpret the core values of Americans and redefine free speech and restrict any speech against Islam.

Should America go down this path, we will be in the same place where the U.K., France, Germany, The Netherlands and multitudes of other countries are now. We, as Americans, could soon find ourselves forbidden by law from saying anything publically against Islam, yet allowing Islamics and their Jihad, via Sharia Law to dominate America and allow our Judeo-Christian values to be supplanted by the demonic book, "**the Koran**." God help us!

We have seen from the Koran and Hadith that the notions of tolerance and peaceful coexistence that Islamic leaders publically suggest **do not** exist, "in fact;"

> "O you who believe (Muslims)! Take not the Jews and Christians for friends, protectors or helpers, they are but friends and protectors of each other. And if any amongst you (Muslims) takes them for friends, then surely he is one of them. Verily, Allah guides not those people who are the (zalimun), polytheists and wrong doers and unjust (Christians and Jews).

The Muslims are quick to accuse the Christians and Jews of being intolerant, yet America has over 3,000 mosques, and as of this date, over 100 under construction, with ten of those being the "**super mosques**," not including the ground zero mosque, which in my opinion will be built as a symbol of Islamic victory and domination.

It is my prayer that America will wake up before we become like the United Kingdom, the Netherlands, France, Germany, Canada and other nations who find themselves in the position of <u>no return</u>, and are now controlled by Islamic law. May God use you after having read this book, that you are now informed of the true facts of Islamic teachings and their wicked ideologies, that you will truly be **salt and light** in an increasingly dark, decaying, world. Our only answer is to turn back to God, and in so doing vote out of office every political leader that will not listen, or refuses to protect <u>our great Constitution and nation</u>.

I SINCERELY PRAY THAT GOD, THROUGH HIS "HOLY SPIRIT," WILL PROTECT AMERICA FROM "THE COMING ISLAMIC INVASION."

Bibliography

Adeney, Maryam, *"Daughters of Islam, Building Bridges with Muslim Women,"* InterVarsity Press, Downer's Grove, IL, 2002.

Al-Araby, Abdullah, *"Islam Unveiled,"* The Pen vs. the Sword Publishers, Los Angeles, CA, 2002.

Al-Hilali, Dr. Muhammad Taqi-ud-Din & Khan, Dr. Muhammad Muhsin, *"Translation of the Meaning of The Noble Qur'an in the English Language,"* King Fahd Complex for the Printing of The Holy Qur'an, Madinah, K.S.A., publication date not listed.

Ankerberg, John & Weldon, John, *"Fast Facts on Islam,"* [What You Need to Know NOW], Harvest House Publishers, Eugene, OR, 2001.

Anonymous, *"Terrorist Hunter,"* Harper Collins Publishers, New York, NY, 2003.

Baagil, Dr. Hassan M., *"Christian Muslim Dialogue,"* Al-Jannat Printing Press, Mt. Holly, NJ, 1984.

Bickel, Bruce & Jantz, Stan, *"Bruce & Stan's Pocket Guide to Islam,"* [A User Friendly Approach], Harvest House Publishers, Eugene, OR, 2002.

Bodansky, Yossef, *"Bin Laden, The Man Who Declared War on America,"* Forum, An Imprint of Prima Publishing, Roseville, CA, 2001.

Braswell, Jr., George W., *"What You Need to Know About Islam and Muslims,"* Broadman & Holman Publishers, Nashville, TN, 2000.

Burke, T. Patrick, *"The Major Religions,"* [An Introduction with Texts], Blackwell Publishers, Cambridge, MA, 1996.

Caner Emir Fethi & Caner, Ergun Mehmet, *"More Than A Prophet,"* [An Insider's Response to Muslim Beliefs About Jews and Christianity], Kregel Publications, Grand Rapids, MI, 2003.

Caner, Emir Fethi & Caner, Ergun Mehmet, *"Christian Jihad,"* [Two Former Muslims Look At The Crusades and Killing in the Name of Christ], Kregel Publications, Grand Rapids, MI, 2004.

Caner, Emir Fethi & Pruitt, H. Edward, *"The Costly Call,"* [Modern-Day Stories of Muslims Who Found Jesus], Kregel Publications, Grand Rapids, MI, 2005.

Caner, Ergun Mehmet, *"Voices Behind the Veil,"* [The World of Islam Through the Eyes of Women], Kregel Publications, Grand Rapids, MI, 2003.

Chapman, Colin, *"Cross and Crescent Responding to the Challenge of Islam,"* InterVarsity Press, Downer's Grove, IL, 2003.

Chapman, Colin, *"Islam and the West,"* [Conflict, Co-Existence or Conversion?], Paternoster Press, Carlisle, Cumbria, UK, 1998.

Copeland, Lynn (General Editor), *"Into the Den of Infidels,"* Living Sacrifice Book Company, Bartlesville, OK, 2003.

Demy, Timothy, *"In The Name of God,"* [Understanding the Mindset of Terrorism], Harvest House Publishers, Eugene, OR, 2002.

Dereksen, David, *"The Crescent and The Cross, The Fall of Byzantium, May 1453,"* G.P. Putnam and Sons, Van Rees Press, New York, NY, 1964.

El Schafi, Abd, *"Behind the Veil Unmasking Islam,"* Pioneer Book Company, Caney, KS, 2002.

Emerson, Steven, *"American Jihad, The Terrorists Living Among Us,"* The Free Press, New York, NY, 2002.

Gabriel, Brigette, *"Because They Hate,"* [A Survivor of Islamic Terror Warns America], St. Martin's Press, New York, NY, 2006.

Gabriel, Mark A. PhD, *"Islam and the Jews: The Unfinished Battle,"* Charisma House, Lake Mary, FL, 2003.

Garlow, James L., PhD., *"A Christian's Response to Islam,"* River Oaks Publishing, Tulsa, OK, 2002.

Gaubatz, P. David & Sperry, Paul, *"Muslim Mafia,"* [Inside the Secret Underworld That's Conspiring to Islamize America], WND Books, Los Angeles, CA, 2009.

Geisler, Norman L. & Salecb, Abdul, *"Answering Islam"* [The Crescent in the Light of the Cross], Baker Books, Grand Rapids, MI, 2001.

Gibb, Sir Hamilton A.R., *"Mohammedanism An Historical Survey,"* The New American Library, New York, NY. 1955.

Gilchrist, John, *"Jam' Al-Quran, The Codification of the Qu'ran Text,"* Jesus to the Muslim, Industrial Press, Benoni, South Africa, 1989.

Goldmann, David, *"Islam and the Bible,"* [Why Two Faiths Collide], Moody Publishers, Chicago, IL, 2004.

Gunaratna, Rohan, *"Inside Al-Qaeda Global Network of Terror,"* Berkley Books, New York, NY, 2002.

Hefley, James & Marti, *"By Their Blood, Christian Martyrs of the Twentieth Century,"* Baker Books, Grand Rapids, MI, 1996.

Hitchcock, Mark, *"Iran the Coming Crisis,"* [Radical Islam, Oil & the Nuclear Threat], Multnomah Publishers, Sisters, OR, 2006.

Hitchcock, Mark, *"The Coming Islamic Invasion of Israel,"* Multnomah Press, Sisters, OR, 2002.

Ibrahim, Ezzeddin & Johnson-Davies, Denys, *"Forty Hadith Qudsi,"* Dar Al-Koran Al-Kareem (The Holy Koran Publishing House), Beirut, Lebanon, 1991.

John, George, *"Operation Crescent Moon,"* [Underground Christians Reaching Muslims in the Land of Mohammad], Pioneer Book Company, Caney, KS, 1994.

Johnson, David Earle, *"Conspiracy in Mecca, What You Need to Know About the Islamic Threat,"* David Johnson Books, Cape Canaveral, FL, 2002.

Johnson, David Earle, *"Princes of Islam,"* [Leaders of the Islamic Conspiracy and Why They Hate Us], David Johnson Books, Pensacola, FL, 2002.

Johnson, David Earle, *"The Land is Still Mine,"* [Should America Give Away God's Land?], David Johnson Books, Alexander, NC, 2004.

Khan, Dr. Muhammad Muhsin, *"The Translation of the Meanings of Sahih Al-Bukhari,"* [Arabic-English, The Hadith, Volumes 1-9], Dar AHYA Us-Sunnah, Al Nabawiya, K.S.A., publication date not listed.

Kruschwitz, Robert B., *"Christianity and Islam,"* [Christian Reflection: A Series in Faith & Ethics, Volume 15], The Center for Christian Ethics, Baylor University, Waco, TX, publication date not listed.

Lewis, Bernard, *"The Arabs in History,"* Oxford University Press, Oxford, England, UK, 2002.

Lindholm, Charles, *"The Islamic Middle East An Historical Anthropology,"* Blackwell Publishers, Cambridge, MA, 1996.

Lindsey, Hal, *"The Everlasting Hatred,"* [The Roots of Jihad], Oracle House Publishing, Murrieta, CA, 2002.

Maalouf, Tony, *"Arabs in the Shadow of Israel,"* [The Unfolding of God's Plan for Ishmael's Line], Kregel Publications, Grand Rapids, MI, 2003.

Marshall, Paul, (General Editor), *"Religious Freedom in the World, A Global Report on Freedom and Persecution,"* Broadman & Holman Publishers, Nashville, TN, 2000.

Marshall, Paul, *"Their Blood Cries Out,"* [The Worldwide Tragedy of Modern Christians Who Are Dying for Their Faith], Word Publishing, Dallas, TX, 1997.

Marshall, Paul, Green, Roberta, Gilbert, Lela, *"Islam at a Crossroads,"* [Understanding Its Beliefs, History and Conflicts], Baker Books, Grand Rapids, MI, 2002.

Martyrs, The Voice of, *"Christian Witness Among Muslims,"* [A Guide to Understanding the Muslim Religion Through the Eyes of Jesus] Living Sacrifice Book Company, Bartlesville, OK, 1994.

Mather, George, A. & Nichols, Larry A., *"Dictionary of Cults, Sects, Religions and the Occult,"* Zondervan Publishing House, Grand Rapids, MI, 1993.

McDowell, Josh & Deedat, Ahmed, *"Was Christ Crucified?"* [A Debate Between Josh McDowell and Ahmed Deedat], Muslim Friendship Ministry, Toronto, Ontario, Canada, 1981.

McDowell, Josh & Stewart, Don, *"Handbook of Today's Religions,"* Thomas Nelson Publishers, Nashville, TN, 1983.

McDowell, Josh, *"The Best of Josh McDowell,"* [A Ready Defense], Here's Life Publications, San Bernandino, CA, 1990.

McManus, Erwin Rafael, *"Seizing Your Divine Moment, Dare to Live a Life of Adventure,"* Thomas Nelson Publishers, Nashville,TN, 2002.

Mordecai, Victor, *"Is Fanatic Islam a Global Threat?"* No Publisher listed Taylor, SC, 1997.

Moucarry, Chawkat, *"The Prophet & The Messiah,"* [An Arab Christian's Perspective on Islam and Christianity], InterVarsity Press, Downer's Grove, IL, 2001.

Musk, Bill, *"Holy War,"* [Why Do Some Muslims Become Fundamentalists?], Monarch Books, Mill Hill, London, UK, 2003.

Newton, P & Haqq, M. Rafiqul, *"Women in Islam,"* The Berean Call, Bend, OR, 1995.

Newton, P. & Haqq, M. Rafiqul, *"Allah, Is He God?"* Muslim Christian Dialogues, Columbia, SC, 1997.

Olasky, Marvin, *"Standing for Christ in a Modern Babylon,"* Crossway Books, Wheaton, IL, 2003.

Parshall, Phil & Julie, *"Lifting the Veil, The World of Muslim Women,"* Gabriel Publishing, Waynesboro, GA, 2002.

Parshall, Phil, *"Muslim Evangelism, Contemporary Approaches to Contextualization,"* Gabriel Publishing, Waynesboro, GA, 2003.

Parshall, Phil, *"The Cross and the Crescent,"* [Understanding the Muslim Heart and Mind], Gabriel Publishing, Waynesboro, GA, 2002.

Pipes, Daniel, *"Militant Islam Reaches America,"* W.W. Norton and Company, New York, NY, 2003.

Poston, Larry A. & Ellis, Jr., Carl F., *"The Changing Face of Islam in America,"* [Understanding and Reaching Your Muslim Neighbor], Horizon Books, Camp Hill, PA, 2000.

Price, Randall, *"Unholy War, The Truth Behind the Headlines,"* [America, Israel & Radical Islam], Harvest House Publishers, Eugene, OR, 2001.

Rhodes, Ron, *"Islam, What You Need to Know,"* [Quick Reference Guide], Harvest House Publishers, Eugene, OR, 2000.

Ridenour, Fritz, *"So What's the Difference?"* [A Look at 20 World Views, Faiths and Religions and How They Compare to Christianity], Regal Books, Ventura, CA, 2001.

Ruckman, Dr. Peter S., *"The Holy Scripture vs. The Holy Koran,"* BB Bookstore, Pensacola, FL, 2001.

Saal, William, *"Reaching Muslims for Christ,"* Moody Press, Chicago, IL, 1993.

Safa, Reza A., *"Inside Islam,"* [Exposing and Reaching the World of Islam], Charisma House, Lake Mary, FL, 1996.

Shorrosh, Dr. Anis A., *"Islam Revealed, A Christian Arab's View of Islam,"* Thomas Nelson Publishers, Nashville, TN, 1988.

Spencer, Robert, *"The Politically Incorrect Guide to Islam and the Crusades,"* Regnery Publications, Washington, D.C., 2005.

Spencer, Robert, *"The Truth About Muhammad,"* [Founder of the World's Most Intolerant Religion], Regnry Publishing, Washington, D.C., 2006.

Timmerman, Kenneth R., *"Countdown to Crisis, The Coming Nuclear Showdown with Iran,"* Three Rivers Press, New York, NY, 2006.

Valentin, Radu, *"Jesus: Friend to Terrorists"*, Living Sacrifice Book Company, Bartlesville, OK, 1995.

Wurmbrand, Pastor Richard, *"Tortured for Christ,"* [30th Anniversary Edition], Living Sacrifice Book Company, Bartlesville, OK, 1998.

Zeidan, David, *"The Sword of Allah,"* [Islamic Fundamentalism from an Evangelical Perspective], Gabriel Publishing, Waynesboro, GA, 2003.

Zwemer, Samuel, M., *"Islam and the Cross,"* [Selections From the Apostle to Islam], P & R Publishing, Phillipsburg, NJ, 2002.

ALLAH IS NOT THE CREATOR GOD OF

THE BIBLE.

GLOSSARY OF TERMS

(Not Exhaustive)

Allah: god in Islam, the moon god of the Arabic world in Muhammad's day, this is a very different god from that of the Bible.

Allah Akhbar: god/Allah is great (greatest); a term of praise in Islam; war cry of Muslims.

Caliph: Title of the ruler or leader of the Umma (Global Muslim Community); the head of the former Islamic Empire; several Caliphs ruled after Muhammad's death; the title was abolished in 1924.

Dar-al-Islam: "House (Realm) of Islam;" Islamic territory ruled by Sharia law.

Dar-al-harb: "House (Realm) of war;" territory ruled by non-Muslims called infidels.

Dar-al-sulh: "House (Realm) of truce;" territory ruled by non-Muslims (infidels) but allied with Islam: also used for terrritory ruled by Islam, but not under Sharia law.

Eid: Arabic for festivity, celebration or feast. Islam celebrates two: Ramadan and the Feast of Sacrifice.

Fatwa: A legal ruling of Islamic law, usually a death sentence.

Hadith: "Report," the musings and sayings of Muhammad, transmitted orally until written down in the eighth century. The Hadith, (published in nine volumes); second only to the Koran and is viewed as the commentary on the Koran.

Hijra: "Emigration," Muhammad's flight from Mecca to Medina in 622 A.D.

Imam: The title of an Islamic mosque's spiritual leader.

Intifada: means "uprising." An uprising by Muslims against non-Muslims who rule a particular country in which the Muslims reside. Considered war against the enemy.

Islam: "Submission" or "surrender."

Jihad: "Holy war," war against all non-Muslims (the infidels).

Jizyah: The poll or head tax prescribed in Surah 9:29, and paid by Christians and Jews (rather than death), thus, submission to Islam.

Kaba: "Cube." The Kaba, cube, or temple where 360 idols were housed before Muhammad's conquest of Mecca in 632 A.D., which is the most venerated object in Islam. Islam believes the Kaba's cornerstone fell from heaven, and that it is the stone on which Abraham was to sacrifice Ishmael (not Isaac). It was in the "Kaba" that Muhammad smashed all the false gods except "Allah."

Kafir: An infidel, one who refuses to submit to Allah, all non-Muslims.

Koran: Also spelled Qu'ran, both are authentic. The compiled verbatim works of Allah as dictated from Gabriel to Muhammad to his friends orally (Muhammad could not read or write).

Mecca: The holiest city of Islam; the place of Muhammad's birth 570 A.D.; its great mosque contains the Kaba stone.

Medina: "City." Short for the "city of the prophet," the second holiest city of Islam; the destination of Muhammad's hijra (emigration) in 622 A.D.; this is the city where the more violent Surahs were supposedly revealed (also known as the yathrib).

Muhammad: "The praised one," also "Ahmed," having the modern day meaning.

Muslim: "One who submits," or surrender (to Allah).

Salat: Muslim daily prayers.

Surah: Also can be spelled "Sura;" a chapter of the Koran as Surah 9:5.

Islam –Recommended Books

1. A Christian Response to Islam, Garlow
2. American Jihad, Steven Emerson
3. Answering Islam, Geisler & Saleeb
4. Behind the Veil, Abd El Schafi
5. Christian Jihad, Caner & Caner
6. Conspiracy in Mecca, David Earle Johnson
7. Cults, World Religions and Occults, Kenneth Boa
8. Fast Facts on Islam, John Ankeberg & John Welden
9. God of Moral Perfection, Felibri
10. Handbook of Today's Religion, Mc Dowell
11. Holy War, Bill Musk
12. In the Name of God, Timothy Demy & Gary P. Stewart
13. Is Fanatic Islam a Global Threat? Victor Mordecai
14. Islam and Jews, Mark A. Gabriel
15. Islam and the Bible, Goldman
16. Islam and the Cross, Zwemer
17. Islam and the West, Chapman
18. Islam at the Crossroads, Marshall, Green & Gilbert
19. Islam in America, Poston & Ellis
20. Islam Revealed, Shorrosh
21. Islam Unveiled, Abdullah Al-Araby
22. Jesus and Muhammad, Mark A. Gabriel
23. Militant Islam Reaches America, Daniel Pipes
24. More Than a Prophet, Caner & Caner
25. Muslim Mafia, Gaubatz
26. Out of the Crescent Shadows, Caner
27. Pocket Guide to Islam, Bickel & Jantz
28. Practical Guide to Islam, Brekel

29. Princes of Islam, David Johnson
30. So What's the Difference? Fritz Ridenour
31. Sword of Allah, David Zeidan
32. The Cross and the Crescent, Parshall
33. The Islamic Middle East, Lindholm
34. The Myth of Islamic Tolerance, Spencer
35. The Truth About Muhammad, Spencer
36. Unveiling Islam, Caner
37. Voices Behind the Veil, Caner
38. What You Need to Know About Islam & Muslims, Braswell
39. What You Need to Know About Islam & Muslims, George W. Braswell, Jr.

Many of these books may be ordered from
Conservative Theological University campus bookstore:
www.conservative.edu and go to bookstore link.
1-800-GO-BIBLE (order by phone)

Islam –Recommended Web Sites

1. www.911truth.org
2. www.americancongressfortruth.com
3. www.americastruthforum.com
4. www.answering-islam.org
5. www.anti-cair-net.org
6. www.blessedcause.com
7. www.cc.org
8. www.danielpipes.org
9. www.geertwilders.com
10. www.hallindsey.com
11. www.isislampeaceful.com
12. www.jihadwatch.com
13. www.peacefulislam.com
14. www.truthsthatfree.com

It is our prayer that you will study—to recognize the enemy of the Gospel of Jesus Christ, then: **warn the world**!

"ISLAM IS NOT TOLERANT!"

Islam –Recommended Videos

1. America, Israel & Islam
2. Holy Land: Christians in Peril
3. Indonesia; Island Jihad
4. Inside the Islamic Mind
5. Islam Religion of Peace?
6. Israel, Islam and Armageddon
7. Obsession, Radical Islam's War Against the West
8. Radical Islam on the March
9. Radical Islam's War Against the West
10. Relentless – The Struggle for Peace in the Middle East

We realize there are many others that are informative; however, we have found these to be extraordinarily educational and accurate.

God bless you as you continue to seek the truth.

Keep informed
www.truthsthatfree.com